Getting to Know Jesus

This book reads like a conversation. It anticipates questions. Makes you glad you were about to ask. And offers keen biblical insight. I couldn't help feeling like I was sitting with a trusted friend over a cup of coffee who was ready to tell a story or answer a question to help me. I recommend this book to anyone on the journey or to anyone helping others on the journey of Getting to Know Jesus.

Pastor Jock Ficken, Executive Director, Pastoral Leadership Institute, Wheaton, IL

Outstanding! Paul has given us a wonderful tool for helping understand the six chief parts of Luther's Catechism from the framework of a relationship with Jesus. I love it! *Getting to Know Jesus* is easy to read and uses simple, contemporary concepts! It is definitely a tool that we will use within the ministry of Concordia. Thank you, Paul!

Bill Tucker, Sr. Pastor, Concordia Lutheran Church, San Antonio, TX

Knowing *about* Jesus is good, but knowing *Jesus* is the real gift. Rev. Paul Schult gives us a refreshing and faithful pathway for knowing Jesus better via the treasures of the six chief parts of Luther's Small Catechism. Using rich relational language and analogies, Paul brings correct doctrine to life and helps us embrace and apply it to everyday life.

Greg Finke, Dwelling 1:14

Pastor Paul Schult is a pastor's pastor—relational to the core with a firm commitment to the enduring truth of God's Word and its applicability to everyday life. This "little handbook" for transmitting those truths to the next generation should find a welcome place in any congregation trying to find the right marriage of doctrine and pastoral care in adult discipleship.

Scott Seidler, Pastor, Concordia Lutheran Church, Kirkwood, MO

Getting to Know Jesus helps the reader see Luther's Catechism in a fresh and exciting way—focused on a God that loves us and seeks to restore us in our relationship with our creator. Drawing on lessons learned from daily life and from modern scholars as well, the book makes deep theological concepts accessible to all. Finally there is a book about the Catechism I can highly recommend to my whole congregation!

Mark Schulz, Pastor, Trinity Lutheran Church, Lisle, IL

Paul has given a fresh framework of relationship for the core teachings of the faith. His contrasts, pithy turns of phrase and jewels of quotes are worth your time. As a pastor who himself prays to know Jesus better and help others to do so, this a fresh tool in that God-designed calling.

Jeff Schrank, Pastor, Phoenix, AZ

Pastor Schult does a fantastic job in sharing the truths of God's love in a simple and straightforward way. This book would be very helpful to people who are introducing a loved one to the Christian faith. The personal reflection questions at the end of each chapter compel the reader not to pass a quiz on content, but to let the word of Christ dwell in them richly. This book is a homerun and I joyfully recommend it.

Tim Klinkenberg, Pastor, St. John Lutheran, Orange, CA

Once in a great while, a book comes along and makes things make sense. *Getting to Know Jesus* is such a book. It is a must-read for anyone seeking to understand who Jesus is and why he wants a relationship with all people. If you are looking for fresh material for your adult confirmation class, or you just want to make the understanding of doctrine more personal for you and your learners, this book is for you. After reading these pages you will come to know Jesus and his desire for you to "live in a deep, genuine, life-giving, and personal relationship" with him.

Joel Koerschen, Executive Director of Education, CNH District, LCMS

Disciples seek to get to know Jesus better each day of their life on earth. This book is a terrific step in the journey for the infant and mature disciple alike. I found this book helped me grow in the core teachings of the Bible and strengthened my faith in the love of Jesus that is shared within these pages.

Greg Griffith, Pastor, Immanuel Lutheran Church, Macomb, MI

As a psychologist, I have spent a lifetime attempting to understand and to mend relationships. As Paul Schult has stated in his excellent book, relationship is the essence of life. Paul goes on to describe the foundational relationship that each of us, either today or sometime in the future, must establish and nurture—the relationship with Jesus. Reading this will greatly assist everyone, no matter where they currently are in the journey with Jesus. I highly recommend it.

Dr. James Osterhaus, Senior Partner, TAG Consulting, Fairfax, VA

Paul Schult brings profound Christian doctrine alive with practical, down-to-earth pastoral insight. *Getting to Know Jesus* is relevant and readable—a great new tool to teach and share the Gospel.

Ted Laesch, Senior Pastor, Chapel of the Cross Lutheran Church, St. Louis, MO

I've known and admired Paul Schult for fifteen years as his friend and consultant. *Getting to Know Jesus* is a superb book. In explaining theology from a highly relational and practical perspective, Paul has taken a subject that is too often overly academic and made it accessible to the average person. I hope this book reaches a large audience, as it certainly deserves it!

Kevin Graham Ford, Principal of TAG Consulting, and author of *The Secret Sauce: Creating a Winning Culture*

I've had the opportunity to use this resource three times to teach adult confirmation. I intend on using it more. Why? It connects the head of faith with the heart of faith! Pastor Schult rightly reminds the reader that being a Christian means more than having the right answers. It's about being in an active, ongoing relationship with the Lord. Using the Six Chief Parts of Luther's Small Catechism, Pastor Schult clearly demonstrates these Biblical truths in a way 21st Century Americans will easily understand. This book is a great resource and long overdue!

Jason Auringer, Pastor, Immanuel Lutheran Church, Wentzville, MO

I have admired Paul as a pastor, teacher, and leader for the past fifteen years while doing life and ministry together. Now, I am so pleased to admire my friend as author. Nobody gets to the heart of the matter quite like Paul. God has blessed him with the gift of making the complex simple, and in so doing, wonderful! This book zeroes in on the ultimate area of life that matters most—knowing Jesus!

Chuck Schlie, Pastor, Messiah Lutheran Church, Weldon Spring, MO

"I've known Paul Schult for ten years, and I can promise you that by reading this book, you'll see a reflection of his heart as a pastor. More importantly, you'll see a reflection of the heart of God. Getting to know Jesus isn't something you do once or even five times. It's a lifelong relationship, and this book will serve as an instrument for you, no matter what stage of that relationship you're in."

Mark Rouland, Pastor, Zion Lutheran Church, Harvester, MO

Getting to Know Jesus

USING THE SIX CORE TEACHINGS OF THE BIBLE TO
GROW IN A DEEPER RELATIONSHIP WITH JESUS

PAUL SCHULT

TENTH
POWER

Elgin, IL • Tyler, TX

TENTHPOWERPUBLISHING
www.tenthpowerpublishing.com

Design by Inkwell Creative

Softcover ISBN 978-1-938840-07-4

e-book ISBN 978-1-938840-08-1

10 9 8 7 6 5 4 3 2 1

To my bride, Beth –

Nothing in my life has helped me grasp the love of Jesus more than you. Through our life together, the Holy Spirit has opened my eyes to the depth of God's love for me in Jesus. It is my great joy and honor to be your husband.

A special word of thanks for great colleagues and friends who read my manuscript and gave me many great insights and suggestions for clarity and accuracy.

Pastor Chuck Schlie and Pastor Don Matzat – My colleagues at Messiah Lutheran Church, along with Pastor Roger Keller and Pastor John Rauh. I love being in ministry with all of you! Thanks for your friendship and passion for Jesus and his mission.

Pastor Ted Laesch – My brother-in-law. I am grateful for your humble wisdom!

Pastor Scott Bruick – This project has felt like the good old days at seminary in our study room, you helping me with my homework!

Pastor Keith Ellerbrock – Thanks for letting me tap into your publishing and writing experience! Your keen eye and your heart for a gospel tone are greatly appreciated!

Jim and Kathe Galvin – Thanks for your friendship, mentoring, and encouragement!

TABLE OF CONTENTS

INTRODUCTION

I HAVE WRITTEN THIS BOOK with one purpose in mind: that you will know Jesus better.

Here is a prayer that the Apostle Paul prayed for the people he knew and loved ... *"I keep asking that the God of our Lord Jesus Christ will give you the Spirit of wisdom and revelation so that you may know Jesus better." (Ephesians 1:17)*

And that is my prayer for you as you read and study this book. In today's world, the words Christianity and Christian have come to mean so many different things that it can be hard to sort it all out. It is easy to be overwhelmed by the many issues involved with Christianity and to miss the most important thing—Jesus.

Along the way of life most people learn a few things *about* Jesus from the Bible, at Church, or from other people. You know a few facts, you can answer a few basic questions, and you get the gist of Christianity. But do you really *know Jesus* in a personal way—in the same way you know other people who are very close to you in life? When you love another person deeply, you probably know a lot *about* the person. But your knowledge goes to a much deeper level than just knowing facts. The more time you spend with someone you love, the more you start to understand their personality, their character traits, their values, and their deep convictions. You can almost predict how they will respond in certain situations; you know what they are thinking by a certain expression on their face. *Knowing about* a person is a critical part of really getting to know them. But the ultimate goal is to *know* the person.

For many people, that's what is missing when it comes to being a Christian: you may know *about Jesus*, but you may never have discovered what it means to *know him*. As you encounter Jesus in the Bible, his desire is for you to know his heart, his mind, and his personality; what he loves and hates, what he values and treasures. I often encourage people to seek having a deep relationship with Jesus.

So that is my prayer, my hope, my purpose—that you will know Jesus better.

"No one has ever seen God, but God the One and Only Son, who is at the Father's side, has made him known." (John 1:18)

RELATIONSHIP LANGUAGE

Here is a quick summary of how I will go about trying to accomplish that main purpose: I will use relationship language to present the six core teachings of the Christian faith. Let me explain very briefly those two things, both relationship language and the six core teachings of the Christian faith.

First, let's consider relationship language. The Bible compares the relationship between Jesus and his people (the Church) to a bride and groom. Jesus is the groom, and the church is his bride.

" 'For this reason a man will leave his father and mother and be united to his wife, and the two will become one flesh.' This is a profound mystery—but I am talking about Christ and the Church." (Ephesians 5:31-32)

God's desire is for you to live in a deep, genuine, life-giving, and personal relationship with Jesus. That is the essence of what it means to be a Christian.

Relationships are a vital part of life. Actually, relationships are the essence of life. Jesus said the two most important things in life are to love God and to love your neighbor. Of all the human relationships in life, God designed the closest and most intimate relationship to be between a husband and wife. So we will talk about all kinds of relationships, but most of all, we'll talk about marriage. And we will look at the six core teachings of the Bible as more than just facts and truths. We will consider them as a means for God to bring you into a deep, profound, and personal relationship with Jesus.

THE SIX CORE TEACHINGS

Throughout Christianity, the six core teachings of the Christian faith have served as a way for the Church to instruct people in the most critical teachings of the Bible. In the Lutheran Church, those six core teachings are explained in a book titled *Luther's Small Catechism* written by Martin Luther. Traditionally, these six core teachings of the Bible are often referred to as the *six chief parts* of the Christian faith. Here is a list of those six core teachings and how each one fosters a relationship with Jesus.

#1 – The Ten Commandments – reveal God's values

#2 – The Apostles' Creed – reveals God's identity

#3 – The Lord's Prayer – reveals how to communicate with God

#4 – Baptism – reveals how to be identified with God

#5 – Confession and Forgiveness – reveal how to be honest with God

#6 – The Lord's Supper – reveals how to commune with God

Doctrine is defined as a set of beliefs. Christian doctrine is a set of beliefs about Jesus based on what the Bible reveals about him. When you begin to study doctrine, it is an intellectual, academic process. And that is very important! It is critical to know the truth, to understand the truth. But as you study these important truths and teachings, don't ever lose sight of the fact that they are a means to an end. God never intended the Bible to only be a resource for academic study. God gave us the Bible to reveal Jesus—so that you may know him, and be saved through faith in him. Don't lose sight of the reality that your life is a journey to know Jesus better. No matter where you have been, what you have done, where you are now—God has one desire for you, to know and love his Son Jesus, to be saved through him.

God's blessings as you begin this process. I pray that the Holy Spirit will use the Word of God to reveal Jesus to you, so that you may know him better.

BE PATIENT

As you read this book, I would encourage you to keep one thing in mind— be patient! It takes a lot of time to get to know another person, and it will take time for you to get to know Jesus. In fact, God intended it to last a lifetime! There are a lot of Bible verses, stories, and concepts referred to in this book. Many of them may be new to you. It will take time for you to become deeply familiar with them. These teachings are very simple and clear, but also very deep and profound. They capture and reveal the heart of Jesus. As you take them to heart and apply them to your life and faith, you will continue to know Jesus better, but it will take time. As you worship, pray, read and study the Bible, and talk with others about these things, you will find that these six core teachings capture the heart of Jesus.

PRAYER

One last word. I love these words from the Bible. I use them as a prayer frequently.

"This is what the Lord says . . . 'Call to Me and I will answer you and tell you great and unsearchable things you do not know.'" (Jeremiah 33:3)

If you are seeking to know Jesus better, pray to him, and ask him to make himself known to you. That is a prayer he loves to answer, and always does!

CHAPTER 1

THE BIG PICTURE
An Explanation of the Gospel – The Six Core Teachings of the Bible

"The fear of the Lord is the beginning of wisdom, and knowledge of the Holy One is understanding." (Proverbs 9:10)

CLIFFSNOTES. HAVE YOU EVER USED THEM? Is it cheating to use CliffsNotes? That was always the question in high school and college, wasn't it? If you aren't familiar with CliffsNotes, they are little booklets that summarize and analyze major literary works in a very condensed format. It's a short cut! Rather than read a 600-page novel, you go to the bookstore and pick up the 30-page summary from our good friend, Cliff. For the most part, my teachers told me it was okay to use CliffsNotes—as long as you were using them to supplement your reading rather than replace your reading. As an English major in college, I really did love to read, and I enjoyed reading novels. But I have to admit there were those times in the spring when an afternoon game at Wrigley Field watching the Chicago Cubs play baseball was a little more than I could resist, and I had to rely on Cliff.

The point is a summary can be a very helpful tool. That's why Martin Luther wrote two books called the *Luther's Small Catechism* and *Luther's Large Catechism*. He understood the importance of a brief summary to help in the task of teaching and comprehending. In the preface to *Luther's Large Catechism* he wrote, *"This much is certain: anyone who knows the Ten Commandments perfectly knows the entire scriptures."*

Even God is a big fan of summaries. That's why he gave us the Ten Commandments, a summary of all God's teachings about life. The Bible is certainly a major literary work—66 books written by a variety of authors over a period of several thousand years. It takes time and work to read, to study, and to apply it to your life. A summary is an incredibly helpful tool, in addition to actually reading the Bible! Jesus summarized the teachings of the Bible for his disciples after He had risen from the dead. *"And beginning with Moses and all the Prophets, Jesus explained to them what was said in all the Scriptures concerning himself."* (Luke 24:27)

In the 1500s in Germany, Dr. Martin Luther wrote *Luther's Small Catechism*—a summary of approximately 30 pages—because parents needed help teaching their children the most important concepts of the Bible. Once the parents and children were well grounded in the main concepts, they could study the stories of the Bible and see the themes played out in the Scriptures and apply them to their lives. Luther also wrote *Luther's Large Catechism*, a longer and deeper explanation for training pastors in the core teachings of the Christian faith.

THE GOSPEL

To know Jesus, the most important thing to understand is something called the gospel. "Gospel" is not a word most people use very often. In the Bible it means "good news." It is the word used to express the central truth of the Bible, the Good News that God is loving, gracious, and merciful. The gospel is the story that in spite of mankind's sinful rebellion against God's authority as our Creator, he sent his Son to pay for our sin. Through the suffering, death and resurrection of Jesus, he restores that broken relationship with him for eternity. Many people use the words of John 3:16 to summarize the gospel: *"For God so loved the world, he gave his one and only Son, that whoever believes in him shall not perish, but have everlasting life."* The gospel is about living in fellowship and harmony with the source of all life. The gospel is about being in step with the author of life. The gospel is about grace, God's undeserved kindness toward sinners. The gospel is about mercy, God saving us from the punishment our sins deserve. The gospel is about new life, being born again and given a new heart.

Here is a list written by Pastor Mark Driscoll that describes the critical difference between religion (man-made spirituality) and gospel (God-revealed spirituality).

1. **Religion** says, if I obey, God will love me. **Gospel** says, because God loves me, I can obey.

2. **Religion** has good people and bad people. **Gospel** has only repentant and unrepentant people.

3. **Religion** depends on what I do. **Gospel** depends on what Jesus has done.

4. **Religion** has the goal to get things from God. **Gospel** has the goal to get God.

5. **Religion** sees hardships as punishment for sin. **Gospel** sees hardship as sanctified affliction (God working to grow my faith).

6. **Religion** is about me. **Gospel** is about Jesus.

7. **Religion** believes appearing as a good person is the key. **Gospel** believes that being honest is the key.

8. **Religion** has an uncertainty of standing before God. **Gospel** has certainty based upon Jesus' work.

9. **Religion** sees Jesus as the means. **Gospel** sees Jesus as the end.

10. **Religion** ends in pride or despair. **Gospel** ends in humble joy.

Here's how Pastor Tim Keller of Redeemer Church in Manhattan explains it:

> *The Bible's purpose is not so much to show you how to live a good life. The Bible's purpose is to show you how God's grace breaks into your life—against your will—and saves you from sin and burdens that you otherwise would not have been able to overcome.*
>
> *Religion is 'if you obey, then you will be accepted.' But the gospel is, 'if you are absolutely accepted and sure you are accepted, only then will you ever begin to obey.'*

Those are two utterly different things. Every page of the Bible shows the difference.

Here is what Tim Keller calls the prayer of the gospel:

> *Dear Lord, I am weaker and more sinful than I ever dared to admit.*
>
> *But through you, I am more loved and accepted than I ever dared to hope.*
>
> *Thank you for . . . paying my debt, bearing my punishment, and offering me forgiveness.*

THE SIX CORE TEACHINGS OF THE BIBLE

When you go on a trip, it's helpful to look at a map and see the big picture of where you are going. This chapter is a brief summary of the six core teachings of the Bible, and how God uses them to bring you into relationship with him, and grow his relationship with you. Each following chapter will unpack one concept in more depth and help you apply it to your own life. Remember, the six core teachings are the pillars of relationship building.

#1 – The Ten Commandments – God's Values

A value is something of worth, a deeply important priority. When you value something, it is very personal to you. You defend it, guard it, promote it, and live it. The stronger a person clings to their core values, the more their actions are governed by those beliefs. A person with strong core values has consistent behaviors that are predictable and steady; they do not change because of circumstances. A person without deeply held core values is very inconsistent, hard to read or predict, and unstable. As you might imagine, it is much easier getting to know a person with deeply held core values. Over time, you see the behaviors regardless of circumstances. It doesn't matter who is watching, what personal gain is at stake, or how much pressure is being applied to a person with strong core values, they don't change. There is something very appealing about a person with strong core values; they stand for something bigger than themselves. They do what they say, and seem to have a strong foundation that creates confidence and certainty even in tough situations. Core values are a critical part of relationships.

Perhaps the best way to discover a person's true values is to watch them over a long period of time. Eventually every person's life is a testimony to their values. If you truly treasure something, your life will be deeply invested in it, consistently, and over long periods of time. If your life doesn't give witness to your values, it's easy to conclude that your words are just talk, that you are saying what you think I want to hear, that you are putting on an act to win my affections, that your values are not deeply held, but put on to gain something you want. That's why time is a great asset when choosing a spouse, and in choosing friends!

When it comes to God's values, he couldn't be clearer than he is in the Ten Commandments. Of all the wonderful parts of God's creation, he boils the truth of life down to ten simple concepts. They are his values, the truths he holds near and dear to his heart. What he loves and what he hates. God isn't interested in trying to impress you. He will never say what you want to hear simply to win your affections. God isn't into playing games. He is up front and clear. He chiseled his values into stone and gave them to the world. They have never changed; and they never will. No revised editions, no addendums, no add-ons! No changes of heart or going back on his Word.

No adapting to culture! They stand the test of time! God's actions have aligned with his values since the beginning of time. They are rock solid, and you can stake your life on them! God's actions are very predictable because they are rooted in unchanging principles of truth. When you understand the Ten Commandments, God's actions will make much more sense to you.

These strong core values of God make it very easy to get to know him! He is steady, unchanging, the same yesterday, today, and forever. God knows that in order for us to know him and to be drawn close to him, his values need to be clearly laid out for us! And so the Ten Commandments reveal the heart of God; what he loves and holds sacred, and what he despises and detests. They define what gives life and what destroys life. Don't mistake God for some wishy-washy, spineless sap, who morphs into someone different depending on who he is talking to, or how he feels on a particular day. God is the same yesterday, today, and forever. He does not change. The words he etched into stone and gave to Moses thousands of years ago are still the same. Jesus said he did not come to change one letter of the law.

When we are drawn close to the heart of God through the gospel, we start to see what a treasure God's commands really are: we start to see that God values life, love, joy, and relationships. When we start to love the things God loves, and hate the things God hates, we know we are being drawn closer to him. Throughout the history of mankind, those who have listened to God's commands and made them the foundation of life have discovered the rich and abundant blessings of his ways.

"Blessed is the man who does not walk in the counsel of the wicked or stand in the way of sinners or sit in the seat of mockers. But his delight is in the law of the Lord, and on his law he meditates day and night. He is like a tree planted by streams of water, which yields its fruit in season and whose leaf does not wither. Whatever he does prospers." (Psalm 1:1-3)

God's truths are a firm foundation that will never be washed away.

#2 – The Apostles' Creed – God's Identity

"What's in a name? That which we call a rose by any other name would smell as sweet." Words spoken by Romeo to Juliet in Shakespeare's tragic play. The quote captures the essential struggle of Romeo and Juliet; the struggle between a person's name and their true identity. In many ways, the two are inseparable. As much as Romeo wanted to change the connection between his name and identity, he could not.

It is amazing how deeply your identity is connected to your name. I often ask students in my classes how they would go about finding a person they had met or seen if they didn't know the person's name. It's quite a quandary! If you know a person's name, you have access to volumes of information about that person. It can be a little frightening to think about how much of your life is "on the record." Things we say, write, do, own— much of it is recorded or documented. If the police suspect you have done something illegal, they have no problem reconstructing much of your life. When potential politicians are vetted, they have their lives laid out for the world to see. It's hard to run away from your past!

When you meet a new person, the first words of introduction are usually your name. In many ways, you are telling them your identity! You are inviting them to get to know you better. If you meet a stranger who approaches you aggressively and inappropriately, chances are that you will refuse to tell them your name. You want to withhold your name to protect yourself. Keeping your identity from a person keeps them at a distance. Knowing your identity allows people to get closer to you. When people lie about their identity, it can be terribly destructive and hurtful. Identity theft has become a big problem in the United States, and it deeply affects the victims whose names are damaged.

I have discovered that one of the greatest offenses is when someone intentionally mischaracterizes another person's name. It is amazing how quickly a few words can undo years of work. It is also amazing to hear how much money large companies will spend to create positive impressions about their name. People spend a lot of time and money to build up a name, and unfortunately, to tear down a person's name.

The deeper two people grow in a loving relationship, the more they know each other's identity—their family background and their life's experiences. In many ways, a person is the sum of all their thoughts, words, and actions. It is immensely important that a husband and wife have a deep understanding of each other's identity. That knowledge draws them closer.

When it comes to having a relationship, knowing a person's name and identity is essential. Because God's greatest desire is to be close to his people, he tells us his name, so we can call on him, refer to him, praise him, and identify him. He didn't have to give us his name! It is a risky proposition! How often do we take his name in vain to curse, swear, and lie? Think of how God's name has been grossly misrepresented by people trying to get rich, get what they want, or justify their evil desires. Think of how God's name is profaned and mischaracterized.

But because he loves us, he gives us his name, his identity. That's the beauty of being born again as a child of God, we take on a new identity; we take on the name of our God. We become his! And his character is bestowed on us; we are declared righteous, forgiven, a new creation, and a child of God. That's why God wants us to know his true identity! So we can be identified with him!

The Apostles' Creed is really nothing more than a summary of God's true identity—who he is and what he has done. Throughout the early years of the Church, leaders got together because God's name was being mischaracterized. Hey, God doesn't like that anymore than you do! So Christians got together to defend God's name, to speak the truth about who God really is! That's why many Christian churches speak the Apostles' Creed in church every week; they are defending the truth and honor of God's name. They are defending his true identity! People speak all kinds of falsehoods about God. The most widely accepted statement defending God's name is the Apostles' Creed.

Just as you depend on people who love you to defend your name, so does God. He gives us his name so we can know him and love him; and then he asks us to defend and protect his name. He is Father, Son and Holy Spirit—three persons, yet one God. The Bible is filled with names that give rich meaning to God's identity: Immanuel, God with us; God's personal name, Yahweh; the Great I Am, often translated as Lord; The God of Abraham, Isaac, and Jacob; The God of Israel; The Lion of Judah; the Prince of Peace; Wonderful Counselor; and the Almighty.

God's identity is on record in the pages of the Bible. His words and actions are there for all to see, and read, and study. He wants to be known and loved! In effect, God says, "Let's get to know each other! Allow me to introduce myself."

#3 – The Lord's Prayer – Communicating with God

"Location! Location! Location!" Those are the three key words for real estate. Likewise, "Communication! Communication! Communication!" are the three key words for relationships. In many ways, relationships are communication! The two are inseparably connected. If communication stops, relationships die. Communication is the lifeblood of any relationship.

Imagine if I told you I was good friends with a famous celebrity. Impressed by the news, you ask, "When was the last time you talked to him?" What would your response be if I told you I have never talked to him? You would think I'm a weirdo, delusional, maybe even a stalker. If you don't communicate with a person, there is no relationship.

Communication is necessary for a relationship, but *good* communication is necessary for strong, healthy, and deep relationships. The result of bad communication is a bad relationship. Two people may be close enough to communicate, yet be in a relationship filled with conflict and tension.

The way we communicate matters! Bad communication creates confusion, doubt, pain, and mistrust. And a lack of trust leads to distance and the breakdown of relationship. You are very familiar with bad communication, and so am I. We all do it. We use communication to hurt, to play games, to guard, to defend, and to mislead. We say one thing, but insinuate something very cynical and hurtful through our tone of voice and body language. We throw out incredibly hurtful words, followed by "I was just kidding! Boy, you are sensitive! Lighten up!"

One of my favorite books is *The Screwtape Letters* by C.S. Lewis. The book is a series of letters from the devil to one of his junior assistants, giving him tips about how to drive a wedge into people's relationships with each other and with God. One of the most powerful techniques is through communication games, always presuming innocence for you and assuming malicious intent for others. It is clear that there is communication that increases conflict and communication that creates harmony. *"Avoid godless chatter, because those who indulge in it will become more and more ungodly."(I Timothy 2:16)*

Part of my job as a pastor is to meet with couples who are engaged to be married. It is always interesting to observe how they communicate with each other, and to talk about the importance of communication. Nothing can make or break a marriage faster than communication. Too often couples in conflict withhold communication as a way of hurting each other. Too often couples use communication to hurt and tear each other down. Husbands and wives that have a deep, rich, loving marriage use communication in ways that build up, encourage, and draw them closer together.

There is no doubt about it—communication matters! God knows that, too! He wants to communicate with his children. He speaks to us very clearly through his Word—the Scriptures. And he invites us to enter into dialogue by calling to him in prayer. The disciples asked Jesus to teach them how to pray so they could learn how to talk to God. And, in response, Jesus gave them The Lord's Prayer. It was a prayer for them to use word for word, but it was also a model; a list of topics God wants to talk about every day! The Lord's Prayer is the perfect model for healthy, productive, deep, and meaningful conversation with God, which draws people closer to God.

Martin Luther explains the spirit of the Lord's Prayer based on the words, "Our Father who art in heaven," saying, "with these words God tenderly invites us to believe that he is our true Father and that we are his true children, so that with all boldness and confidence we may ask him as dear children ask their dear father."

We are all inclined to focus our conversations on ourselves; what I want, what I need, what I don't like, what I want changed or fixed. And that is certainly part of communication! But it is not the only part! Conversation also means listening, considering, reflecting, empathizing, gaining new perspectives, considering other thoughts and insights. Those kinds of conversations cause relationships to grow stronger—for friends, for families, for spouses, and most of all between God and his children.

#4 – Baptism – Commitment: Let's Get Serious!

"Will you marry me?" Those are exciting words—aren't they? Maybe you have experienced the joy of asking or being asked that question. Maybe you haven't had that experience yet, but you eagerly hope for that day. Or maybe the topic of marriage is bittersweet because of past disappointment or pain. Whatever the case, the process of getting engaged is a very important part of the process leading to marriage.

It brings up the all important "C" word—commitment. Some people avoid commitment. What if someone better comes along? What if I change my mind? What if we fall out of love? It is understandable to think that making a commitment restricts your life. But the truth is, commitment and love working together open the door for the kind of deep relationship God created us to experience in marriage.

When two people agree to marry, they acknowledge that they love each other deeply and intend to commit exclusively to each other for the rest of their lives. That exclusive commitment creates a relationship of total openness and trust. In order to truly open your heart and engage fully in a relationship with another person, you need to trust that they are committed to you and will never turn against you. The more trust you have in a person, the more you are willing to open your heart to love. Love leads to commitment, and commitment feeds love!

Think for a moment about the process of getting engaged. What if getting married didn't involve any legal action? What if you didn't need a license; no vows, no witnesses, no formalities, no records—no commitment? What if marriage was only one person asking another person to be married, and then an affirmative answer? Could you imagine how unstable the institution of marriage would become? Society has placed certain legal requirements on marriage, in order to encourage people to have a certain level of commitment. Once you take that step there are responsibilities. Commitment creates an environment of trust!

Engagement is really one more step of commitment that allows a relationship to continue growing deeper. A promise, a very expensive ring, public announcements, your picture together in the newspaper; it all adds up to commitment. With that promise, both individuals are able to start *acting* on that commitment. Plans begin to be made. Where will we live? How will we manage our money? Who will we visit for Christmas? Commitment allows people to begin meshing their lives together and acting with confidence, knowing that the future is secure.

God desires that same kind of confidence from his children. He wants us to be certain that he is completely committed to us. He wants us to know he will never leave us nor forsake us. Have you ever noticed that the most prominent promise from God in the Bible is that he will be with us? That's because he doesn't want us to be tentative, insecure, and worried about his love for us. He doesn't want us to go to sleep every night wondering if

God still loves us because we had a bad day. He doesn't want us to wake up thinking we need to make amends for yesterday by living a better life today. He doesn't want us to think he leaves us when we are bad, giving us the cold shoulder. He doesn't want us be motivated by fear and scorekeeping. He wants us to rest secure in his love. A person's true beauty comes out when they are deeply loved and can live with confidence.

God knows that anxiety breaks down relationships. When a person is anxious, they tend to engage in behaviors that are unproductive and hurtful. God doesn't want that! He wants people to be assured of his grace.

That's why he gives us baptism. It involves a physical marking—like a ring—so we can be sure of our identity as a child of God. God goes on the record and lets it be known we belong to him! He will never leave you. He will never reject you. You can open your heart completely to God and know that nothing will ever stop him from loving you. God knows that your true beauty will shine when you find your confidence and strength in his love! God is committed to you, because of his love! *"And surely I will be with you to the end of the age." (Matthew 28:20)*

#5 – Confession and Forgiveness – Unconditional Love: Let's Get Honest!

I'm fascinated by the television show *Law and Order*. I love observing human nature, how people deal with inner personal struggles, and how they struggle to own up to the truth. The characters reminded me of how much I struggle owning up to my sins. Facing up to the truth of our own behavior is one of the hardest things to do in life. If you don't believe it, just watch people in the courtroom. It is incredibly difficult to admit the truth and face the consequences of our behavior. One of the moments that is most intriguing is when people plead guilty and are forced to confess their crime. People whisper, shade the truth, stall, minimize, justify, and excuse. Judges practically have to threaten them with contempt of court to get them to speak the truth! Judges know how important it is to own up to the truth. It must be done! There can be no exceptions. You cannot give people an out—or they will certainly come back and take it. They must go on record and own up to their crime.

"When I kept silent, my bones wasted away through my groaning all day long. For day and night your hand was heavy upon me; my strength was sapped as in the heat of summer. Then I acknowledged my sin to you and did not cover up my iniquity. I said, 'I will confess my transgressions to the Lord'—and you forgave the guilt of my sin." (Psalm 32:3)

Oh the power of admitting the truth of our sins! One of the most powerful verses in the whole Bible is this: *"Now we know that whatever the law says, it says to those who are under the law, so that every mouth may be silenced, and the whole world held accountable to God." (Romans 3:19)* God already knows everything about us! He knows the deepest, darkest thoughts and sins of our hearts. But God knows the power of us coming clean with him, and being cleansed by his forgiving love. He wants us to realize the depth of our sin—and to own up to it!

It's no wonder Jesus said, *"You will know the truth and the truth will set you free," (John 8:32)* and, *"Surely you desire truth in the inner parts." (Psalm 51:6)* God knows that confessing the truth of our sins brings us closer to him. That's the way it works in a marriage; the more honest and open you can be with your spouse, the closer you will grow together. When sincere, loving hearts repent and turn away from sin, and gracious forgiveness is extended, relationships grow deeper in love. Owning up to our sins opens the door to the power of God's grace!

That's what God desires, too! God knows the power of true confession. And he knows how denying sin can harden the heart and cause love to grow cold. The more we accommodate sin and allow it to settle into our hearts and lives, the more it separates us from our Savior, Jesus. Tolerated sin soon grows into comfortable sin and then into intentional sin. And that is a dangerous place to be! Where there is intentional, planned sin, there is a hard heart.

But when a person genuinely acknowledges his sin and admits it, God gives grace and forgiveness; he gives the person a new heart, restored by God. *"Create in me a pure heart, O God, and renew a steadfast spirit within me . . . The sacrifices of God are a broken spirit; a broken and contrite heart, O God, you will not despise." (Psalm 51:10, 17)* Truth is foundational in any relationship!

#6 – The Lord's Supper – Intimacy: Let's Get Close!

Intimacy. That's a powerful word! It means "marked by very close association, contact, or familiarity." It involves closeness to another person, both physically and emotionally. For a husband and wife, intimacy is very important—physically and emotionally. The two are designed to go together. God created it to work that way; physical intimacy should be directly related to emotional intimacy.

There are certain social graces that demonstrate this truth. When you encounter a total stranger, you keep a little distance. With an acquaintance, you might shake their hand; with a close friend, you may embrace or kiss the cheek. For a family member, you might embrace and even say, "I love you." When you hold your child, you might caress his or her face. And for a husband and wife, the touches become even more intimate. These physical touches match the emotional intimacy that exists. If you caress the face of a stranger, you might be accused of inappropriate behavior, maybe even assault. Touch someone else's child and you might be in trouble. You don't walk up to strangers and ask them to marry you.

We need intimacy! We need to be close to other people. We need emotional closeness, and we need physical closeness. But God gives us some very clear guidelines about intimacy, especially in the sixth commandment, which will be covered in chapter 2. By God's design, sexual contact is reserved for one person, your spouse, who is the one person you are closest to emotionally and physically. When those lines that God has established are violated there are tremendous problems and confusion; broken hearts, abuse, rape, pedophilia, molestation, etc. When physical closeness happens without emotional closeness, it creates trouble and heartache.

God desires to be close to you as well. He desires to be close to you in every way. That's why Jesus said the greatest commandment is to love God with all your heart, soul, mind, and strength. The Bible has a lot to say about how God dwells among his people—physically and emotionally. He desires real closeness with you! That's what the Lord's Supper is all about. In a very divine and mysterious way, the body and blood of Jesus Christ inhabit the bread and wine at the Lord's Supper. As God's people eat and drink the bread and wine, they also eat and drink the body and blood of Jesus. The body and blood of Jesus are absorbed into your flesh—the two become one. That's as close as you can get to Jesus on this side of heaven! But for that kind of physical closeness to take place, God asks for emotional closeness as well. The Lord's Supper is for those people who are baptized children of God, who sincerely repent of their sins, who believe that Jesus has forgiven their sins, and who recognize the real presence of Jesus' body and blood at the Lord's Table. Communing with Jesus at his table is a powerful experience! That's what Jesus intended it to be! And when all six relationship dynamics are at work in a person's life, God rejoices at being close to you his child!

It's All about Relationships: Six Core Teachings

That's it! Those are the six foundational dynamics of relationships. Just as learning the multiplication tables is essential to proficiency in math, learning about relationships is essential for life! Relationships don't happen by accident. They don't happen automatically. Relationships take time, energy, and work. My basketball coach used to have a saying, "Practice doesn't make perfect. Perfect practice makes perfect." You can practice the wrong things and get a result that is far from perfect. God has given us the answer for relationships, and it is called the gospel. As you discover how Jesus creates relationships with his people, you will discover life the way

God intends it to be—rich, full, and abundant! Gospel-based relationships make life work! Now it's time to dig a little deeper into each of these concepts so we might know Jesus better!

PERSONAL REFLECTION

Spend some time reflecting on the following Bible passages and questions. Take some time to consider your thoughts, what you feel God might be revealing to you. Then spend some time in prayer, asking God to give you his Holy Spirit to help you in the process of getting to know him better.

1. Read each of the following Bible passages several times. Reflect on the words and consider what God is saying to you through them. In the space below, write down a few notes about your thoughts.

"I keep asking that the God of our Lord Jesus Christ, the glorious Father, may give you the Spirit of wisdom and revelation so you may know him better." (Ephesians 1:17)

"The fear of the Lord is the beginning of wisdom, and knowledge of the Holy One is understanding." (Proverbs 9:10)

Jesus said, "I am the good shepherd; I know My sheep and My sheep know Me . . . My sheep listen to My voice; I know them, and they follow Me." (John 10:14, 27)

2. Think about the spiritual journey you have taken throughout your life. Reflect on the various phases of your life: childhood, high school, college, and adulthood. Think of people who had a spiritual influence on you. Think of times you felt close to God. Reflect on what God might be revealing to you at this point in your life. Write down some of your thoughts in the space below.

3. Pray; ask God to open your heart and mind to know him better.

CHAPTER 2

THE FIRST CORE TEACHING
GETTING TO KNOW JESUS THROUGH THE TEN COMMANDMENTS
God's Values - Ten Truths That Give and Govern Life

"We know that the law is good if one uses it properly." (I Timothy 1:8)

A FRIEND OF MINE COMMENTED about a pastor he knew. People used to say, "He preached the gospel, but you could tell he didn't like to." If you pay close attention, you start to notice what motivates a person, don't you? Everyone can remember a teacher who seemed to almost enjoy punishing his students, and it just didn't seem quite right. There are other people in positions of authority who really are deeply concerned about the people under them. For that person, rules are a tool to help teach, keep order, and to benefit the whole group or community.

Laws and rules are good—if they are used properly. But if they are misused, they can be cruel and harsh. I think that is part of the reason so many people have a bad reaction when they hear the words, "The Ten Commandments." We have all experienced a person who abuses authority, people who are more interested in feeling powerful than they are in helping people. They use rules to oppress people instead of using them to benefit people. It's understandable to have a certain amount of tension when it comes to authority and rules. It is natural for people who experience abuse of power to cast that same expectation on God and to think that the Ten Commandments are oppressive and harsh, and that God is nothing more than power hungry.

RESISTANCE TO AUTHORITY

In 1966, the St. Louis Cardinals built a new ballpark and named it Busch Memorial Stadium. There is a story that the owner of the Cardinals, August Busch, wanted to name it Budweiser Stadium, but the city officials would not allow him to name it after a beer. Frustrated by their answer, he named it Busch Memorial Stadium after their family name. But shortly after the new stadium was opened, August Busch introduced a new beer to the market: Busch beer. I guess he got his way!

When the new Busch Stadium was built in 2006 a similar conflict happened. The city had an ordinance that advertisement signs were not allowed on the outside of the new stadium. Facing the situation of losing millions of dollars in advertising costs, the designers of the stadium got around the ordinance by making a huge sign that faced the outside of the stadium, but was offset by one foot so it was located inside of the building framework. Technically, it was not "on" the outside of the building.

Fascinating! Those stories remind us of our human nature, how easily we can find a way around any rule, and how much we hate being told what we can and cannot do. People have a natural resistance to rules and authority, even if we know they are good for us! God is in the challenging position of being God, which means he has authority over all creation. He makes the rules, but not because he has some twisted need for power. God is holy and perfect, and so are his laws! His laws are merely an extension of his nature, perfect in every way. *The Ten Commandments are not merely ten rules, as much as they are ten words from God that summarize all of his truths that govern life.* When the word "law" appears in the Old Testament, it is usually the word "Torah" which refers to the first five books of the Old Testament. The Torah is the story of God's Ten Words played out in history. God gave us the Ten Commandments as a summary, a way of remembering, teaching, and applying God's truths in our lives. If we use God's laws properly, they have a way of bringing great blessing into our lives and into the world.

THREE USES FOR GOD'S LAW

The Bible presents the three proper uses for God's law: a curb, a mirror, and a guide.

1.   A Curb – God's law keeps people on the path of life.

God knows that we have a way of running off the road of life and crashing into things. That's why he put a curb on the road of life called the law. When we bump into God's law, it keeps us from driving off the road into disaster. The more common name for this is conscience. *"Indeed, when Gentiles, who do not have the law, do by nature things required by the law, they are a law for themselves, even though they do not have the law, since they show that the requirements of the law are written on their hearts, their consciences also bearing witness, and their thoughts now accusing, now even defending them."* *(Romans 2:14-15)*

Conscience is a gift from God, something given to all people. It is an instinct inside that says it is wrong to kill another person or steal something that belongs to someone else, to lie, or to cheat. Just like a road curb keeps order and safety in neighborhoods and communities, so God's laws help keep moral order and safety in the world.

2.   A Mirror – God's law shows us our sin.

This is the greatest purpose for God's law, to help us realize God's holiness and our sinfulness. You probably have several mirrors in your home so you can see for yourself how you really look. It's not easy to tell someone else they have broccoli between their teeth or a coffee stain on their shirt. But a mirror never lies! Likewise, it's not easy for other people to tell us when we are *morally* flawed. That person risks being the object of our anger, resentment, and defensiveness. It's easier to just be quiet. But God's law never lies! And it is never quiet! If we look at God's perfection and holiness, it doesn't take long to see we don't match up. We sin!

The upcoming statement is perhaps the most common misperception about Scripture. This is one of those assumptions we make about God's Word, but if we actually open the Bible and read it, we won't find it! Are you ready? Here it is! *God did not give us his laws so that we could earn his love and favor by obeying them!* It is a natural assumption to make, because that's the way we usually function as human beings. When people are nice to us, we love them. When people are not nice to us, we dislike them. But that reality does not hold true for God. He loves all people unconditionally! He cannot love anyone more, and he cannot love anyone less. His love is not dependent on our behavior! If you remember only one thing from this chapter, remember this . . . *The Ten Commandments have nothing to do with earning God's favor!*

If you have a Bible that you use on a regular basis, I would encourage you to highlight the following passage in your Bible. *"Now we know that whatever the law says, it says to those who are under the law, so that every mouth may be silenced and the whole world held accountable to God. Therefore no one will be declared righteous in his sight by observing the law; rather, through the law we become conscious of sin." (Romans 3:19-20)*

God doesn't give us the law to beat us over the head and make us feel bad. He doesn't give us the law to exert his authority and to make himself feel powerful. He does not lord his holiness over us. He gives us his law so we can see the reality of our sin, and find peace and comfort in his mercy and grace. His law leads us to the gospel! If we try to use the law to gain God's favor, there are only two possible flawed outcomes. We have a false sense of security, that we're pretty good people compared to all the bad people in the world, so God must think we're okay. Or we are overwhelmed with despair. "God could never love me—I'm too sinful."

Now go back to your Bible and highlight this passage. *"But now a righteousness from God, apart from law has been made known, to which the Law and the Prophets testify. This righteousness from God comes through faith in Jesus Christ to all who believe. There is no difference, for all have sinned and fall short of the glory of God and are justified freely by his grace through the redemption that came by Christ Jesus . . . (28) For we maintain that a man is justified by faith apart from observing the law." (Romans 3:21-24, 28)*

The PURPOSE of God's law is to lead us to the righteousness of Jesus, our Savior. And as we read before, if we use the law properly . . . it is very good!

3. A Guide – God's law shows us the way to go.

The first two purposes for God's law are for all people! But the third use is really only for those who have a personal relationship with Jesus, for those who believe in him as their Savior and Lord. For those who love Jesus, the law also becomes a guide for the best way to live for God. No, we can never be perfect! We sin every day in our thoughts, words, and actions. But God's law teaches the difference between right and wrong, and encourages us to seek the blessings of living God's ways.

TWO TABLES

The Ten Commandments are a summary of all God's truths. But even the Ten Commandments can be broken down one more step into two great commandments. *"Teacher, which is the greatest commandment in the Law?" Jesus replied: "'Love the Lord your God with all your heart and with all your soul and with all your mind.' This is the first and greatest commandment. And the second is like it: 'Love your neighbor as yourself.' All the Law and the Prophets hang on these two commandments." (Matthew 22:36-40)* Jesus summarized the Ten Commandments by putting them into two groups. Commandments one through three, the relationship between God and his people, are summarized as the first and greatest commandment to love God. Commandments four through ten, the relationship between a person and his neighbors, are summarized as the second greatest commandment to love your neighbor as yourself.

NUMBERING THE TEN COMMANDMENTS

If you read the Ten Commandments in the Bible—in either Exodus 20 or Deuteronomy 5—you will see that they are listed and called the Ten Commandments. But they are not numbered! Different groups have numbered them differently. For instance, *Luther's Small Catechism* divides coveting into two commandments: numbers nine and ten. Many other Protestant churches divide "no other gods" and "no idols" into two commandments, known as one and two. The Jews started with the first line which is actually a proclamation of gospel rather than a command, "*I am the Lord your God who brought you out of Egypt, out of the land of slavery.*"

The Ten Commandments are referred to in the Greek language as the "Decalogue," meaning ten words. If you look at them as The Ten Words, instead of The Ten Commandments, perhaps the Jewish numbering system is the best option. The first word is a statement of fact – God is the one who saves us. Therefore, listen to his words!

THE FIRST COMMANDMENT

"I am the Lord your God. You shall have no other gods." What does this mean? We should fear, love, and trust in God above all things.

When speaking about the Ten Commandments, Dr. James Nestingen, a professor of theology at Luther Seminary, talks about each commandment as God's "bare minimum." In other words, it is the starting point for each truth. You can spend a lifetime digging into the depths of each commandment, but this is the bottom line bare minimum.

The commandments begin with the bottom line reality that you are a creature, which means that you were created; you have a Creator. Because we are creatures, we must have a god. Every creature chooses something or someone to worship. There is something or someone in this life that you will die for, aspire to, sacrifice for, bow down to, or serve. People make just about anything into a god—good things and bad things: money, sex, power, success, fame, pleasure, themselves, family, church, or a job. But at the end of the day, every one of those gods demands sacrifices. People sacrifice their honor, integrity, time, family, morals, and even life itself.

There is only one God who actually saves people. The God of the Scriptures is the only God who provided the sacrifice for every one of us. God sent his only Son Jesus to take our place, to take our punishment, and to deliver us from sin and death. God knows that following him is the only way to fullness of life, the fullness of life that he created us to know, now and eternally. The God of the Bible is the one and only true God, the Creator of heaven and earth, and the Lord of all creation. To him all human beings are accountable.

THE SECOND COMMANDMENT

"You shall not misuse the name of the Lord your God." What does this mean? We should fear and love God by avoiding cursing, swearing, using satanic arts, lying, or deceiving by his name. Instead, we want to call upon his name in every trouble, offering prayer and praise and giving thanks.

If you are going to have a relationship with God, at the very least you must know his name. Have you ever been caught in a situation where you didn't know a person's name? It's awkward and embarrassing. It doesn't work very well to have to rely on, "Hey you!" And it's awkward to try and introduce them to another friend. God tells us his name (the Apostles' Creed – chapter 3) so that we can know him, call on him, speak to him, speak about him, and introduce him to other people. But he also expects the same courtesy we ask of others with our own name; please don't misuse it! God doesn't want us to use his name to curse, lie, or deceive. Why is it that we call on God's name to back up our words? If we let our yes be yes, and our no be no, no one would have any reason to doubt us. God gives us his name so we can live in relationship with him. It is our duty to honor and respect his name.

THE THIRD COMMANDMENT

"Remember the Sabbath day by keeping it holy." What does this mean? We should fear and love God so that we do not despise preaching and his Word, but instead hold it sacred and gladly hear and learn it.

The third and final necessity of having a relationship with God is to spend time with him. If you are going to have a real, genuine, meaningful relationship with God, you need to spend time interacting with him—speaking, listening, reflecting, thinking, praising, and worshipping. The word "Sabbath" means rest. The greatest rest a person can experience is stopping from his labors to spend time with God; it is rest for the soul. And resting from our labors is a great reminder that the world goes on without us. God is God; we are not!

Psalm 1 is an introduction to the 150 chapters in the book of Psalms, which is a collection of songs and prayers for use in worship. *"Blessed is the man who does not walk in the counsel of the wicked or stand in the way of sinners or sit in the seat of mockers. But his delight is in the law of the Lord, and on his law he meditates day and night. He is like a tree planted by streams of water, which yields its fruit in season and whose leaf does not wither. Whatever he does prospers." (Psalm 1:1-3)*

That's why we should not despise preaching and God's Word, but instead hold it sacred and gladly hear it and learn it. God's Word is life! Quite often I hear people say, "I can be a Christian without going to church." As you might imagine, those words can be a little frustrating for a pastor. Of course, having a pastor suggest that you go to church may seem self-serving. But the truth of God's Word is that those words are spiritually dangerous. Here's the danger: those words contain a little truth, but they are dripping with an underlying sentiment that is not what God desires. Technically, a person can go to heaven without going to church. But make no mistake about it, God's will is for people to assemble regularly to worship!

A person could also say, "I can be married and not love my spouse." Likewise, that statement is technically true. But it has an underlying sentiment that is deeply troubling. A marriage based on that perspective will be cold, impersonal, and shallow. It will be so much less than God created marriage to be. And so it is with worship. God desires a rich, deep, meaningful relationship with you. That relationship is fostered in worship, where God's Word is celebrated, honored, preached, and proclaimed. There is a reason God gave us the Third Commandment! He wants us to assemble for worship and find true rest for our souls in his presence. (The concept of worship will be unpacked further in chapters 7-9.)

Commandments one through three represent the first table of the law and the most foundational law of life, living in loving relationship with God. A person could grow in understanding and knowledge of those concepts for a lifetime because of their depth and wonder and glory. Just as a husband and wife grow in love through experiencing life together, so we discover the depths of God's love as we experience it in our day-to-day lives.

THE FOURTH COMMANDMENT

"Honor your father and mother." What does this mean? We should fear and love God so that we do not despise or anger our parents and other authorities, but honor them; serve and obey them; love and cherish them.

The Fourth Commandment begins the second table of the law, living in loving relationship with your neighbors. Relationships have such a profound effect on life. They are the flavor of life, the color of life. And the art of living in relationship begins at home. When God created mankind, he created us male and female. His master plan was that we would become part of his creative process of bringing new human life into existence. Adam was created from the dust of the ground and God breathed into him the breath of life. God created Eve by taking Adam's rib and forming a woman. God could have populated the earth by continuing to create from the dust of the earth. But instead, he created us male and female and said, *"For this reason a man will leave his father and mother and be united to his wife, and the two will become one flesh." (Genesis 2:24)* Through marriage, God calls a husband and wife into the divine activity of creating new life. The family is the place God designed for new human life to be conceived, brought forth, protected, taught, loved, nurtured, nourished, and raised to adulthood.

The Fourth Commandment is all about the starting place for human life and human relationships, the home! Here, godly authority is given, received and learned. *One of the primary foundations of human relationships is honor!* Human life is to be honored and cherished. That's where parents come in! Children learn from their parents that human life is God's greatest value! Children learn from their parents that God cherishes the human life and soul more than anything else in creation. For children, parents become a living picture of God. Although all parents are imperfect and fall far short of God's glory, their primary task as parents is to point their children to their true heavenly Father, through his Son Jesus.

When children are raised in a home where they are cherished, valued and deeply loved, they learn to do the same. As they are raised in the fear, knowledge, and grace of God, they learn to honor their parents, because they are honored as precious children of God! And when children grow up learning to cherish people, they carry that attitude out into the world. Homes filled with honor, respect, and love produce confident children. Not arrogant; confident!

Earthly authority is a gift of God, which he uses to deliver his blessings to people. (Read Romans 13.) God works through people, even though we are imperfect sinners. And knowing how to respect and honor authority is vital to a child's well-being in this world. A child that is cherished and valued, and taught to cherish and value others, will go out into the world treating others with respect; he will expect the same thing from others. When that is multiplied by hundreds and thousands of households, it produces communities of thriving, confident people. Where there is honor and respect for human life, people are confident to go out and do great things working, serving, learning, and living.

But what happens when a child grows up in a household where he is degraded, humiliated, and resented? What does it do to the heart of a child when she is told by her parents that she is an annoyance, a bother? It is crushing to a child's spirit if a parent tells him that he should have never been born. That child grows up afraid. He goes out into the world timid, expecting to be useless and abused. Put these children together, and they are drawn to oppressive, abusive, hostile situations. Their lives often become less than they could or should be, certainly not the full and abundant life God desires!

The fourth commandment is so fundamental to life. And parents do well to give great thought and prayer to the task of having a household where human life is honored and cherished. Without this dynamic in place, the remaining commandments really don't matter much.

THE FIFTH COMMANDMENT

"You shall not murder." What does this mean? We should fear and love God so that we do not hurt or harm our neighbor in his body, but instead help and support him or her in every physical need.

Have you ever walked through a place where you felt threatened? A dark alley, a run-down neighborhood with high crime rates, a street filled with an angry crowd or mob? Being in a situation where you fear for your safety is very uncomfortable. There is stress, fear, and worry. We tend to be tense, nervous, and shaky. It's hard to think clearly and function normally. Imagine if you were in a situation where your safety was constantly at risk. Think of a child living in a war zone. Being in that kind of situation stifles life. It restricts work, creativity, production, and service. When our lives are threatened, life is less than God intended it to be. God puts the highest premium on human life; it is the crown of his creation. That's why the next commandment is "Do not murder." Human beings are created in God's image, and their lives are absolutely sacred to him. If neighborhoods and communities are filled with people looking out for each other, protecting, guarding, and helping each other, then people can live in safety and live life to the fullest! Safety brings productivity, comfort, fearlessness, and activity!

Murder is the antithesis of God. God is the Lord of life! He creates! He restores! Death is God's enemy. God's Word has a lot to say about life. He wants us to value human life as much as he does! Therefore, God tells us it is our duty to help protect and guard our neighbor's safety, not just our own. That's why the church historically has taken strong stands against things like abortion, euthanasia, suicide, and embryonic stem cell research. You can read the official Lutheran Church—Missouri Synod positions on these and other topics on the website www.lcms.org. Under the theology tab is a heading called "CTCR Documents" which stands for Commission on Theology and Church Relations. The booklets on these topics are Bible studies and guidelines for dealing with these issues in society and life.

THE SIXTH COMMANDMENT

"You shall not commit adultery." What does this mean? We should fear and love God so that we lead a sexually pure and decent life in what we say or do. Husbands and wives should love and honor each other.

If people are going to live in a community helping, serving, protecting each other, and living in relationships, there need to be some boundaries in those relationships. Different kinds of relationships call for different kinds of boundaries. Not all relationships are the same!

Sexuality is an incredibly powerful part of life. The feelings, emotions, and sensations of sexual contact are incredibly powerful in affecting human behavior. All people need and crave physical and emotional contact. Like anything else in creation that has immense power, it can be the source of great good or great evil.

Sex is a beautiful part of God's creation when it is practiced in the context God designed for it. But sexual relationships outside of God's plan can bring great pain and suffering. Many people have come to me for pastoral counseling because of the intense pain of a broken relationship that involved sexual relations: divorce, adultery, or pre-marital sex. Quite a few people told me that this kind of pain was greater than any physical pain they have ever experienced. There's a reason for that—God designed sexual activity to take place in marriage, a relationship commitment that is supposed to last a lifetime "until death parts us." The breaking off of sexual relationships results in one of two things: scars or calluses. Scars are the result of a wound that eventually heals. But doctors know that scar tissue is never the same as healthy tissue. Scar tissue has no sensitivity; it is hardened and inflexible. A callus is a hardened surface that develops in a spot that endures too much friction. It prevents injury—but it also dulls the senses. A callus is hard and coarse, and it stops sensitivity and feeling. When emotional scars and calluses cover the human heart, eventually it becomes difficult to sense and feel true love. Only God's Holy Spirit can truly heal a wounded heart!

God's plan for marriage and sex is spelled out in the Bible. It is a plan that avoids scars and calluses, keeping the heart sensitive, strong, and healthy; this is a perfect place for love to grow.

"For this reason a man will leave his father and mother and be united to his wife, and they will become one flesh. The man and his wife were both naked and they felt no shame." (Genesis 2:24-25)

God's plan . . .

1. **Leave mother and father:** The marriage relationship is to be closer than the parent/child relationship. This can be very difficult emotionally for children and parents. Too often adult children stay closer to their parents than to their spouses, or parents come between their adult children and their spouses.

2. **One man—one woman:** This is God's design for creating new life, nurturing that life, and raising it.

3. **Get married:** I am referring to a public ceremony with witnesses, documentation, and public statements of commitment. Contrary to the statements of many people, that little piece of paper called a marriage license really does matter. It matters when it is a deed to a house, a court order, or a contract. And it matters in a marriage. Love and commitment go together.

4. **Sexually united:** Once a fortress of love and commitment has been built around your heart and around your husband/wife relationship, then sex becomes what God intended, a powerful gift from God to deepen your relationship. Sexual intimacy creates an experience that connects two people together in heart, mind, and body.

"I praise You because I am fearfully and wonderfully made."(Psalm 139:14)

God's creation of the human body is an amazing thing. When a male and female engage in a sexual relationship, the emotional, physiological, and psychological reactions are so intimately woven together that the bond is difficult to break. God wired us that way. *"Do you not know that he who unites himself with a prostitute is one with her in body? For it is said, "The two will become one flesh." (I Corinthians 6:16)* A sexual union between a man and woman connects them at a level that is hard to completely comprehend. It is never really possible to disconnect completely. That's why God is telling us, *don't give yourself away in a way that you can't get yourself back.* You can't undo a sexual relationship.

The bottom line is that God knew what he was doing when he created us male and female! He knows what he is talking about when it comes to sexual relationships! His plan works, because he created us that way! The right boundaries when it comes to sexual relationships create situations where people thrive. Protected by commitment and faithfulness, people are confident, secure, loved, and able to live for others. That's why God gives us boundaries in relationships, so marriage is honored and sexual sins don't destroy people. The emotional scars from sexual sins are difficult to heal. The only thing that is strong enough is the perfect love of Jesus Christ, the one who can forgive sin and heal any wound.

"Above all else, guard your heart, for it is the wellspring of life." (Proverbs 4:23)

THE SEVENTH COMMANDMENT

"You shall not steal." What does this mean? We should fear and love God so that we do not take our neighbor's money or possessions, or get them in any dishonest way. Instead, we should help him or her to improve and protect his or her possessions and income.

If you are going to live in this world, you're going to need some stuff! You need stuff to cook with, to fix things, to play with, to wear, to work with, and to enjoy. That's just the way life is. And if you are going to have stuff, you need a place to keep it, and the confidence to know that your stuff is safe, and that people aren't going to steal it. God gives us the Seventh Commandment to protect our money and property, as well as that of our neighbor.

God knows we need stuff. In fact, God wants us to have stuff! He just doesn't want our stuff to get in the way of the things that really matter in life: faith, people, relationships, and most of all, the Kingdom of God. God doesn't want us to worry about stuff, or let the pursuit of it ruin our lives.

Jesus said, "So do not worry, saying 'What shall we eat?' or 'What shall we drink?' or 'What shall we wear?' For the pagans run after all these things, and your heavenly Father knows that you need them. But seek first his kingdom and his righteousness, and all these things will be given to you as well." (Matthew 6:31-33)

"People who want to get rich fall into temptation and a trap and into many foolish and harmful desires that plunge men into ruin and destruction. For the love of money is a root of all kinds of evil. Some people, eager for money, have wandered from faith and pierced themselves with many griefs." (I Timothy 6:8-10)

God's Word warns us about materialism, the worship of things. But he wants us to have stuff and enjoy it! And he wants us to help our neighbor defend and protect his property. If everyone is looking out for their neighbor, and everyone is confident their stuff is safe, they are free to venture out into the world and do great things! If our stuff is safe, we can come home at the end of the day and rest.

THE EIGHTH COMMANDMENT

"You shall not give false testimony against your neighbor." What does this mean? We should fear and love God so that we do not tell lies about our neighbor, betray him, slander him, or hurt his reputation, but instead defend him, speak well of him, and explain everything in the kindest way.

This is when things start to get a little difficult. The Sixth Commandment dealt with one of the strongest temptations for every human being: sexual sins. In my opinion, the Eighth Commandment is the only one that presents the same level of temptation: sins of the tongue. *"The tongue also is a fire, a world of evil among the parts of the body. It corrupts the whole person, sets the whole course of his life on fire, and is itself set on fire by hell." (James 3:6)*

It is so tempting to distort the truth, to gossip or slander, or to tear down someone's reputation. It's quick. It's easy. And it's almost impossible to be held accountable. It's so easy to claim, "I never said that! That's not what I meant! You misunderstood me." The tongue can be so destructive. One of the restraints of sexual sins is that they require time: proactive effort, work, deception, and scheming. But sins of the tongue can happen in an instant, so quickly and easily. God knows that to thrive in this world, we need to have a good name, a good reputation. What a difference it makes when you walk into a room and everyone assumes you are a good person! It's incredibly difficult to overcome a room full of people who expect you to be a bad person. No one trusts you. No one gives you the benefit of the doubt; people give you no room to try. They rush to judgment, giving you a short leash. It takes twice as much work to get half as much done. Everything is an uphill battle.

I think Martin Luther's words in his explanation on this commandment are as hard to follow as any of God's teachings: *explain everything in the kindest way.* How tough is that? Give everyone the benefit of the doubt. "Maybe he's just having a bad day." "Let's give her another chance." "I've seen him be much more positive than that." It's not easy! But that's what God asks of us. God knows how much better life works when we are all working to guard and defend each other's name as well as we can. It doesn't mean we don't speak the truth. It doesn't mean we don't deal with sin and injustice. It means our judgment is tempered with grace and love. It means we speak the truth in love. It means we search for the kindest words instead of the harshest words.

NINTH AND TENTH COMMANDMENTS

"You shall not covet your neighbor's house." What does this mean? We should fear and love God so that we do not scheme to get our neighbor's inheritance or house, or get it in a way which only appears right, but help and be of service to him in keeping it.

"You shall not covet your neighbor's wife, or his manservant or maidservant, his ox or donkey, or anything that belongs to your neighbor." What does this

mean? We should fear and love God so that we do not entice or force away our neighbor's wife, workers, or animals, or turn them against him or her. Instead, we should urge them to stay and do their duty.

To covet means to desire enviously. Envy means painful or resentful awareness of another person's advantages. Those are some powerful words! I had the opportunity to go to a maximum security prison with a friend of mine to help with a Bible class. On the way to the prison, I asked my friend how a person gets to the point of committing murder or any other violent felony. He said he had talked to quite a few inmates about that very question. The answer usually had to do with two things: 1) drugs; and 2) obsession. A person would consider a crime, and then they would think about it more and more and more. They would start to scheme, imagine doing it, and then make plans. Gradually, more and more of their mental attention was spent thinking about actually doing it. Finally the line between thinking and doing was so thin, they finally carried out their intention.

That's a pretty common way for Satan to work. An idea that initially repulses us begins to seem more and more acceptable over time. Obsession wears down our conscience! It doesn't have to be something criminal. Envy can lead to a multitude of sins. Eventually we can rationalize just about anything. One of my favorite quotes was spoken by Pastor Rick Warren of Saddleback Church. He said, "Given the right circumstances, any person is capable of any sin." That saying is so true. Any time you see a horrific crime reported on television, instead of self-righteous judgment, our response should really be, "there but by the grace of God go I." Given the same circumstances, you might do the same thing. If you had grown up in an abusive home, if you had been neglected or abandoned, if you had been treated with brutal violence, who knows what you might do? It certainly doesn't excuse sin! But it should warn us away from the trap of spiritual arrogance and pride. So what's the antidote to covetousness and envy? Contentment.

"But godliness with contentment is great gain." (I Timothy 6:6)

When we are content with God's blessings, we stop comparing and stop desiring what other's have. We start to see other people's advantages with gratefulness and joy instead of envy and anger. God never promised that we would all have the same blessings. I saw a quote once in a school classroom that said, "Fairness isn't everyone getting the same thing. Fairness is everyone getting what they need." God knows what we need—and that's exactly what He gives us. God knows what a terrible place the world can be when people are painfully envious of other's advantages. And he also knows how blessed life can be when people are content and glad for God's blessings in other people's lives.

CONCLUSION

The Ten Commandments are God's values—what God loves and what God hates. He loves the positive side of each commandment, and he hates the negative. Here is a review of the things he loves: 1) worshipping him alone; 2) uplifting his name through our prayers and praises; 3) spending time with his people; 4) the honoring and respecting of authority; 5) holding human life sacred; 6) practicing sexual purity and boundaries in marriage; 7) protecting each other's property; 8) preserving a good name and reputation; and 9 and 10) living with contentment.

Here is a review of the things he hates: 1) worshipping idols and false gods; 2) misusing his name; 3) distancing ourselves from him by neglect; 4) rebelling against authority; 5) committing murder; 6) committing adultery 7) stealing 8) gossiping and slandering 9) coveting and envying your neighbor's things.

That's it! What a clear and upfront list of values! And here's the cool part; the Bible gives us God's account of how these values play out in life. The Bible records the pain and suffering of rebelling against God's commands, and the joys and blessings of following his commands. The Ten Commandments are a summary of the full counsel of God. They are a framework, a template to view all of God's teachings. Everything comes back to these ten words.

As you grow in your knowledge of God's values, repent of the sin in your heart and life, receive the forgiveness of Jesus, and are guided by the truth of God's Ten Commandments, you will be drawn closer and closer to your Creator.

PERSONAL REFLECTION

1. Read over the following Bible passages several times. Reflect on the words and consider what God is saying to you through them. In the space below, write down a few notes about your thoughts.

    "Jesus replied, 'Love the Lord your God with all your heart and with all your soul and with all your mind. This is the first and greatest commandment. And the second is like it: Love your neighbor as yourself.'" (Matthew 22:37-39)

    "Love does no harm to its neighbor. Therefore love is the fulfillment of the law." (Romans 13:10)

    "If we claim to be without sin, we deceive ourselves and the truth is not in us. If we confess our sins, God is faithful and just and will forgive us our sins and purify us from all unrighteousness." (I John 1:8-9)

2. Spend some time reflecting on your relationships—with family, friends, coworkers, and neighbors. Do you hold grudges? Do you honor and cherish people? Are you petty? Are there some conflicts you need to resolve . . . some people you need to apologize to and ask for forgiveness . . . some people you need to forgive? Write down some of your thoughts.

3. Pray for God to give you his Holy Spirit to help you heal broken relationships through his love.

CHAPTER 3

THE SECOND CORE TEACHING
GETTING TO KNOW JESUS THROUGH THE APOSTLES' CREED – GOD'S IDENTITY

Part I – God the Father – Yahweh, Your Creator

GOD KNOWS YOU PERFECTLY, and he wants you to know him, his true identity. The word used to describe God's nature is *Trinity*, which means one God in three persons. It's possible to use some analogies to try to explain that concept, but they all fall short. The nature of God is something that transcends human logic. We can't even come close to understanding the human psyche! How could we possibly fathom the nature of God?

The concept of the Trinity is a mystery. All we can do is state what the Scriptures tell us: God is one. But he is three persons, coequal, and eternal: Father, Son, and Holy Spirit. This concept is a stumbling block for many people. The inability to explain this rationally is one reason some people don't believe the Bible is true. I don't have a problem with this one, because of what I said before; I don't understand myself! Why would I expect to understand the nature of God? There is a lot in this world that I don't understand rationally. I know that science holds many answers about God's creation. But we can never wrap our minds around emotions or human behavior. And we will never be able to fathom all the mysteries of God's identity, either. There is something that we can do, though—we can get to know God deeply! We can know and love other human beings deeply, and we can know and love God deeply as well! In order for that to happen we need to know God for who he really is. Here are the three key identifiers of who God is:

1.   God the Father: Yahweh, the Creator

2.   God the Son: Jesus, the Redeemer

3.   God the Holy Spirit: Counselor, the Sanctifier

The full depth of a person's identity cannot be communicated quickly or easily. We try to introduce people and capture the essence of who they are. We write obituaries, introductions, profiles, and even biographies. But a person's full identity can't really be grasped apart from the story of their life. God's identity can't truly be known apart from his story recorded in the Bible. There is no better way to know God than to read and study the Bible; it is his story. When you read his story, you will discover his identity: Father, Son, and Holy Spirit.

Evidently, God thinks that identity is very important. Two of the Ten Commandments have to do with honoring a person's name and identity. The second commandment is God's request for people to honor his name and his identity, by not misusing it, but by using it to honor him through prayers and praises. The eighth commandment is God's request for us to honor and protect the name and reputation of our neighbors. God knows how difficult it can be to overcome the challenge of being mischaracterized by another person. It takes years to develop a good name, and only a quick moment for a slanderous lie to destroy your good name.

After God's entire story of salvation was played out through Jesus Christ, the fullness of the Trinity was revealed: Father, Son, and Holy Spirit. The Apostles were charged with the task of proclaiming God's true identity and his work of salvation! The Apostles defended God's true identity against many false teachers. And as the New Testament church grew over the first few centuries, the church fathers wrote "creeds"—clear, concise, accurate statements that profess the true identity of the God of Scripture. In many Christian churches, the Apostles' Creed is still recited regularly, to confess, defend, and honor the identity of the one true God. It gains its name because it is based on the teaching of the Apostles. It summarizes what the Bible says about the identity of God. Martin Luther wrote an explanation to each of the three parts of the creed: Father, Son, and Holy Spirit.

THE FIRST ARTICLE – GOD THE FATHER

"I believe in God the Father Almighty, maker of heaven and earth." *What does this mean? I believe that God has made me and all creatures; that he has given me my body and soul, eyes, ears, and all my members, my reason and all my senses, and still takes care of them. He also gives me clothing and shoes, food and drink, house and home, wife and children, land, animals, and all I have. He richly and daily provides me with all that I need to support this body and life. He defends me against all danger and guards and protects me from all evil. All this he does only out of fatherly, divine goodness and mercy, without any merit or worthiness in me. For all this it is my duty to thank and praise, serve and obey him. This is most certainly true. (Luther's Small Catechism)*

Dr. James Nestingen highlights three words in Martin Luther's explanation of the First Article to summarize the essential nature of God the Father: 1) gift; 2) only; and 3) duty.

GIFT

If there is one word in the Bible that is vital to understanding God's heart, the best choice might be the word "gift." The opposite of a gift is a wage. What's the difference between a gift and a wage? A gift is something freely given as an expression of love and gratitude. Gifts are all about expressing love, and building relationships. A wage is something that is earned, expected, and deserved. Wages are contractual, business, impersonal; they have little to do with love or relationships. By "confessing" the words of the Apostles' Creed, we are proclaiming that every good blessing in life is a gift from God. We are also saying that all good things in life are not things that we have earned or deserve. That's really saying something! If we really believe it, that reality should affect our attitude about life. Think about this. Is everything you have in life a gift from God? Or is it all the result of your hard work, what you deserve from God? Every blessing you have in life is a gift from God, because he loves you.

One of the jobs of a parent is to teach a child the proper way to give and receive gifts. Gifts are an important part of life and an important expression for people who love each other. Parents spend time teaching their children how to receive gifts. You probably do this without giving it much thought. And what is the biggest time for giving and receiving gifts? That's right—Christmas! Just picture the scene. It is Christmas Eve. All of your extended family is gathered together sitting in a large circle in Grandma and Grandpa's living room. The adults are on chairs on the outside of the circle, and the children are mostly on the floor in the middle where everyone can see them. The presents are opened one by one. And finally the moment of truth comes—it's time for your child to open his present from Grandma and Grandpa in front of the whole family. You are a little nervous. How will your child respond? Will he be gracious and polite . . . or rude and inconsiderate? How do you want your child to respond to his gift? You probably know all too well what you don't want your child to say: "I already have that!" "Is that all?" "That's not really what I wanted!" "I'm too old for that."

You would much rather hear things like, "Wow—this is awesome!" "Thank you so much for even thinking of me!" "I love it!" "This is the best gift I've ever gotten!" "I can't wait to play with this!" And then it would be just perfect if, without prompting, they went over and gave Grandma and Grandpa a big hug and told them thanks for the great gift. What a difference!

One reaction almost takes the joy out of giving a gift! The other attitude makes it a joyful experience. One of the things I like to ask my children is, "What's the alternative to a gift?" The alternative is not a different gift, the alternative is nothing! If we expect nothing, then any gift is a joy. If we expect something, it takes away from the idea of it being a gift, and turns it into a wage. When it comes to gifts, attitude is everything!

When it comes to giving gifts, there is something much more important than the object that is given. That something is a relationship between the giver and the receiver. We give gifts in part because a person we love might need or enjoy a particular object. But even more, we give gifts because we love, and we want to express that love in a tangible way. Gifts can be very special when they come from the heart, when the gift giver takes time to understand who you are, what you value and love, what really means something to you and takes the time to figure out just the right gift. And even if the gift isn't what you expected, wanted, or needed, the expression of love has a powerful way of drawing you closer to that person. You deserve nothing, and yet someone who loves you very much made a sacrifice to give you a gift. Gifts draw people closer together in love.

"Every good and perfect gift is from above, coming down from the Father of the heavenly lights, who does not change like shifting shadows." (James 1:17)

"Which of you fathers, if your son asks for a fish, will give him a snake instead? Or if he asks for an egg, will give him a scorpion? If you then, though you are evil, know how to give good gifts to your children, how much more will your Father in heaven give the Holy Spirit to those who ask him!" (Luke 11:11-13)

When we begin to realize that everything in this life is a gift from God, then our lives are marked by gratitude! When we realize God has given us a mind capable of solving problems, and bodies to perform work, then the blessings of our labor are not our deserved wages but a gift from God! That's what we confess in the first article of the Apostles' Creed, "God has made me and all creatures, and has GIVEN me . . . " When we truly believe that all the blessings of life are gifts from God, we are humble, grateful, and filled with joy. This reality is the foundation for a joy-filled, happy life. If you live in the reality that everything you have is a gift from God, your life will be in step with God, like an instrument in tune making beautiful harmony. For the person who sees the blessings of life as a wage that he has earned from God, it will forever be a life lacking contentment, peace, joy, and gratitude.

ONLY

The second key word is our statement of belief about what motivates God to give us so many rich blessings. He does this, "ONLY out of fatherly, divine goodness, and mercy." Like a father, God loves his children, and loves giving them good gifts. But unlike any earthly father, God is divine, perfect! His love is always perfect and his gifts are always perfect! It's not because we are such great children that God blesses so richly. It's because his love is divine and perfect! Some of the most beautiful acts of love on earth happen between a parent and child. When we see beautiful acts of sacrifice and love, only one word can describe it; it's ONLY because she is your child. You are God's child and he loves you deeply! It's the ONLY reason he pours out his love and blessing on you.

DUTY

When a person wins the lottery, what do you expect them to do with the winnings? Wouldn't you expect them to share some of their blessings? If a lottery winner told the world, "I plan to spend every last dollar on myself. I don't plan on sharing one red cent of it," you would be shocked! How rude! How selfish! For those who have been richly blessed, there is a bit of a duty to be generous, to share.

That's why the third key word is "duty"—because of God's goodness, kindness, and abundant blessings, it is our duty to "thank and praise, serve, and obey him." I have a paperweight on my desk with a quote from Garrison Keillor etched into the glass that says, *"Thank you, God, for this good life and forgive us if we do not enjoy it enough."* What a great quote! It captures the spirit God intends for us—a spirit of joy, gratitude, and blessing! That's the heart of God the Father. He is our Creator, and he loves pouring out rich blessings into our lives, like a father who enjoys giving good gifts to his children. By confessing the first article of the Apostles' Creed, you are confessing this as the true reality for your life!

There are many other attributes of God the Father that will give you a deeper understanding of his heart. The stories of the Bible demonstrate those attributes. But this summary gives you the essence of God's heart; he is gracious, slow to anger, abounding in mercy and steadfast love. You will learn more about God's heart as you read on.

PERSONAL REFLECTION

1. Read over the following Bible passages several times. Reflect on the words and consider what God is saying to you through them. In the space below, write down a few notes about your thoughts.

    "Be joyful always; pray continually; give thanks in all circumstances, for this is God's will for you in Christ Jesus." (I Thessalonians 5:16-18)

    "This is how God showed his love among us: he sent his one and only Son into the world that we might live through him. This is love: not that we loved God, but that he loved us and sent his Son as an atoning sacrifice for our sins." (I John 4:9-10)

"And he (God) passed in front of Moses, proclaiming, 'The Lord, the Lord (Yahweh), the compassionate and gracious God, slow to anger, abounding in love and faithfulness, maintaining love to thousands, and forgiving wickedness, rebellion and sin.'" (Exodus 34:6-7)

2. Spend some time reflecting on the blessings God has given in your life. It is easy to think only about your problems and things that aren't going the way you want. Jot down some of the things God has graciously given to you—a job, good health, family or friends, wealth, safety, a great nation/community, safety, and his unconditional love. Ask God to help you live a life of gratitude in all circumstances.

3. Pray for God to give you his Holy Spirit to help you be joyful, grateful, and generous with your blessings.

CHAPTER 4

THE SECOND CORE TEACHING
GETTING TO KNOW JESUS THROUGH THE APOSTLES' CREED – GOD'S IDENTITY

Part II – God the Son – Jesus Your Savior

"**I** BELIEVE IN JESUS CHRIST, his only Son, our Lord, who was conceived by the Holy Spirit, born of the Virgin Mary, suffered under Pontius Pilate, was crucified, died, and was buried. He descended into hell. The third day he rose again from the dead. He ascended into heaven and sits at the right hand of God, the Father Almighty. From thence he shall come to judge the living and the dead." *What does this mean? I believe that Jesus Christ, true God, begotten of the Father from eternity, and also true man, born of the Virgin Mary, is my Lord, who has redeemed me, a lost and condemned person, purchased and won me from all sins, from death, and from the power of the devil; not with gold or silver, but with his holy, precious blood and with his innocent suffering and death, that I may be his own and live under him in his kingdom and serve him in everlasting righteousness, innocence, and blessedness, just as he is risen from the dead, lives and reigns to all eternity. This is most certainly true.*

Jesus is God's only Son—our Redeemer. In order to understand the essence of who Jesus is, the first step is to understand what Jesus saves us from; this is the concept of sin. The word "redeem" literally means "to buy back." What does it mean that Jesus redeemed us from sin and death? To understand that, you have to understand the concept of sin.

SIN – WHY DO WE NEED A SAVIOR ANYWAY?

The most essential and fundamental message of the Christian faith is really rather offensive. "You need a Savior!" "Who, me? A Savior from what? I don't feel like I need to be saved from anything!" The truth is, you need a Savior from yourself! Sin has a consequence—an inescapable death beyond our own powers. The Bible describes the story of mankind's first fall into sinfulness. Genesis 3 covers The Fall (the fall into sin). Genesis 4-11 explores the hopelessness and helplessness of mankind under sin. And in Genesis 12, God makes a covenant with Abraham to save mankind from sin.

Sin is rebellion against God and disobedience to his will. God created the heavens and the earth, and he is the ultimate authority! His creation is perfect in every way and his ways lead to life. Rebellion and disobedience are sinful, and sin leads to death; both physical death of the flesh and spiritual death of the soul. Spiritual death is eternal separation from God. The first man and woman God created, Adam and Eve, ate from the tree of the knowledge of good and evil. They disobeyed God. They sinned, and human nature became corrupt. The sons and daughters of mankind took on the fallen sinful nature of their parents.

"Therefore, just as sin entered the world through one man, and death through sin, and in this way death came to all men, because all sinned." (Romans 5:12)

Original Sin: that is the name given to the sin people have from conception. Sin is a part of human nature; we have a natural bent away from God, an inclination to rebel against him and resist his authority. We have a natural desire to be God ourselves, instead of submitting to the authority of the one true God. Actual sin, in contrast, is the name given to our sinful actions. This is how most people think of sin, something you do that is wrong. But the Bible talks about sin being something much deeper that permeates what we think, say, and do. Our natural inclinations are sinful.

"Surely I was sinful at birth, sinful from the time my mother conceived me." (Psalm 51:5)

(Jesus said), "You have heard that it was said to the people long ago, 'Do not murder, and anyone who murders will be subject to judgment.' But I tell you that anyone who is angry with his brother will be subject to judgment . . . You have heard that is was said, 'Do not commit adultery.' But I tell you that anyone who looks at a woman lustfully has already committed adultery with her in his heart." (Matthew 5:21-22, 27-28)

Because of The Fall involving Adam and Eve, all people are sinful. No one is righteous before God. People are not good by nature. They are not inclined to be in-step with God and do his will. People are born hostile to God and are rebellious against his authority. The result is that sin puts a separation between God and mankind. God will not allow sin to be in his presence—if he did, heaven would also be corrupted by sin, suffering, and death. Our sinful condition must be fixed; we need a Savior!

Satan's greatest desire is to separate us from God eternally. Satan is the source of evil, as he hates God! Although he is powerless against God, Satan has one tactic in the battle of good versus evil. Satan wants to capture the thing that is nearest and dearest to God's heart—you! The centerpiece of God's creation and the object of his affection is mankind! He created us in his image so that we can live in a loving relationship with him. God loves relationship! He is love! Nothing breaks God's heart more than people who turn their backs on him, embracing sin and evil and eternal death.

The picture of judgment day is one of the greatest misperceptions of mankind. Many people imagine God seated on the judgment throne. As each person comes forward, God weighs their good deeds against their bad deeds and decides whether or not their deeds have earned them eternal life or death. That's hardly the picture God paints in the Bible.

"Therefore, no one will be declared righteous in his sight by observing the law; rather through the law we become conscious of sin . . . For we maintain that a <u>man is justified by faith, apart from observing the law.</u>" (Romans 3:20, 28)

The Bible portrays judgment day as people rejecting God, literally choosing sin and death. Many people would rather be their own master in hell than submit to God's authority in heaven. Some people will choose to reject God's goodness, and cling to their own sinful desires. Rather than submitting to God's authority and receiving his gift of eternal life, they will rebel, cling to their sins, and receive eternal death.

WHO IS JESUS CHRIST?

That's the definitive question for all mankind. Your answer to that question changes everything. When Jesus asked Peter, "Who do you say that I am?" Peter answered, "You are the Christ, the Son of the living God." (Matthew 16:15-16) One of the best answers to this question is in the book of Colossians. *"He (Jesus) is the image of the invisible God, the firstborn over all creation. For by him all things were created . . . He is before all things, and in him all things hold together. And he is the head of the body, the church; he is the beginning and the firstborn from among the dead, so that in everything he might have the supremacy. For God was pleased to have all his fullness dwell in him, and through him to reconcile to himself all things, whether things on earth or things in heaven, by making peace through his blood, shed on the cross." (Colossians 1:15)*

That says it all! All the fullness of God dwells in Jesus Christ.

HIS NAME

The literal meaning of the name Jesus is "the one who saves." *"She (Mary) will give birth to a son, and you are to give him the name Jesus, because he will save his people from their sins." (Matthew 1:21)* The word "Christ" is a title that means "anointed." It is the title for an office. "The anointed one" means God's chosen Savior for the world. Christ is the Greek word used in the New Testament for anointed. "Messiah" is the Hebrew word used in the Old Testament to describe God's anointed Savior. The name "Jesus Christ" identifies him for his primary purpose, to be God's anointed Savior providing mankind deliverance from the power of sin. Jesus did many other things on earth; but his mission from God was to pay the price for sin, and to reconcile people back to God.

HIS ESSENCE

As confessed in Martin Luther's explanation of Jesus' identity, Jesus is 100% true man and 100% true God. *"I believe that Jesus Christ, true God, begotten of the Father from eternity, and also true man, born of the Virgin Mary, is my Lord."* How can this be? We don't know! It doesn't make logical sense, but it is the truth that God reveals to us in the Bible. We can never understand this fully, but we can observe it, marvel over it, and praise God for it!

Because he was true God, Jesus was conceived and born without sin, able to live a perfect life in our place and be the perfect sacrifice for our sins. Because he was true man, he was able to take our place, to die our death, and to make atonement for our sin. The four gospels in the Bible (Matthew, Mark, Luke, and John) document the divine and human attributes of Jesus.

This issue was the focus of many false teachings and heresies in the early church, and throughout the past 2000 years of church history. Many unorthodox churches have claimed that Jesus was only man or only God. Many people today believe Jesus actually lived here on earth and died on a cross—but they still think he was only a man, merely a good teacher.

Many people reach that conclusion apart from the Bible, for the Bible clearly identifies Jesus as God himself. Those who believe Jesus was only a teacher face the challenge of reaching the conclusion that Jesus was crazy for claiming to be God.

HIS ROLE

Introductions are helpful tools. Before a guest speaker takes the microphone, an introduction provides you advance knowledge of his identity and a better understanding of his message. It's also helpful for another person to introduce a speaker. Speaking about yourself can be a little uncomfortable. Because Jesus is the central figure in the history of the world, the person upon which every person's eternity is based, God put together a rather lengthy introduction to get people's attention.

God introduced Jesus for about 3,000 years through a nation—Israel. In effect, God said, "Watch the history of Israel unfold, and you will come to know the identity of God, the heart of God, and most of all, the identity of the Messiah." God made a promise to Abraham that he would be the father of a great nation. They would be "set apart" from all the other nations of the earth. Through this nation—their history, their rituals, their positions of authority, and their worship, God would be introducing Jesus. There wasn't any one metaphor that God could use to fully capture the identity of Jesus. So God used a multitude of people, events, and lessons to capture as much of Jesus' identity as possible. That way, when Jesus showed up, people would recognize him as the Messiah.

The three greatest *offices* in the Old Testament that help introduce Jesus are: Prophet, Priest, and King. These three offices were occupied by central figures in Israel's history.

1. *Prophet* – A prophet's primary role was to speak the Word of God.

Whenever God had a message of warning, of rebuke, of comfort, or of promise, he would speak through a prophet. As you might expect, many times the prophets' messages were not very popular. Generally speaking, the prophets were persecuted, hated, and rejected. But they spoke God's Word with great resolve. The many prophets of the Old Testament helped introduce a primary part of Jesus' identity—God's greatest prophet, who not only spoke the Word of God, he was the Word of God. *"In the beginning was the Word, and the Word was with God, and the Word was God. He was with God in the beginning... The Word became flesh and made His dwelling among us." (John 1:1-2, 14)*

When Jesus began his public ministry of preaching and teaching, the people marveled at his words. Jesus spoke with authority they had never heard before. That's because Jesus didn't just know God's Word, he was and is God's Word. Jesus is the *author* of all life! It's no wonder he spoke with such great authority.

2. *Priest* – A priest's primary role was to offer sacrifices for God's people.

The priests of Israel worked in the temple, regularly offering sacrifices so people's sins could be forgiven. As you might imagine, priests were more popular with the people. They offered good news, the forgiveness of sins. The priests also helped introduce Jesus who would be God's perfect priest. Jesus didn't offer animal sacrifices. Jesus was the Lamb of God who shed his own blood to pay for our sins once and for all. The book of Hebrews says that once Jesus sacrificed himself, priests were no longer needed!

3. *King* – A king's primary role was to rule over God's people.

The kings of Israel had many important jobs, to lead the military in guarding the nation, to set up systems and laws that provided for the welfare of the Israelites, and to administrate all of those systems. If the king did his job well, there was peace, prosperity, and freedom. If a king failed to do his job well, there was unrest, hardship, persecution, and the threat of foreign invasion. The tasks of the kings of Israel introduce another critical part of Jesus' identity; he was to rule over God's kingdom. But Jesus doesn't rule by the power of the sword. Jesus rules with truth, love, and wisdom. God's laws are always perfect; his wisdom is beyond human comprehension; and his ways lead to peace, prosperity, and freedom. Jesus is God's perfect King!

HIS OWN CLAIMS

One of the hardest things for a person in a position of authority to do is announce their own authority. If you are a parent, and you find yourself telling your children that you have authority and that you are in charge, it is probably a sign that you don't have control! Good leaders exercise their authority quietly, lovingly, wisely, and only in the best interest of those under their authority. They don't do it to show off, feel powerful, or feed their ego. Jesus was in that awkward position of not only having authority, but having "all authority in heaven and on earth." How exactly do you tell people you are the Son of God? How do you announce that you are the Savior of the world? Not an easy task. Remember, most people resent authority. Proclaiming your authority is usually a fast track to stirring up resentment and hostility. When you read the Bible, pay close attention to how Jesus deals with this issue of claiming to be the Son of God. Jesus wasn't in the business of answering people's questions; Jesus was more interested in leading a person to discover who he was.

In effect, Jesus "says things without saying them." He infers. He hints. He suggests. He allows room for people to come to their own conclusions. The best kind of authority is the kind people recognize and honor without having to be told. Some authority figures command respect by their presence, their influence, their attitude, and their actions. There are a few great instances where Jesus claims to be the Messiah, but he does it in a way that allows people to make their own conclusions. Luke 4:14-30 is the story of Jesus teaching for the first time in the synagogue in his hometown of Nazareth. Knowing that the people viewed him as a carpenter's son, not the Messiah, Jesus handles the situation indirectly. Jesus stands up in the synagogue, and reads a passage from the Old Testament—Isaiah chapter 61 —a prophecy about the Messiah. After the reading, Jesus says, "Today this scripture is fulfilled in your hearing." Can you just imagine the reaction of the religious leaders? "What did he just say? Was he claiming to be the Messiah?" Jesus' critics only resented him more. But those who were inclined to believe were drawn even closer.

In Matthew 11, John the Baptist is in prison and wonders if Jesus really is the Messiah. John sends some of his followers to ask Jesus. Jesus doesn't respond by saying "yes" or "no." He tells the followers of John to go tell him what they have seen, again quoting Isaiah 61: *"The blind receive sight, the lame walk, those who have leprosy are cured, the deaf hear, the dead are raised, and good news is preached to the poor."* Jesus says yes, by telling them the prophecies about the Messiah are being fulfilled in him. He says yes without saying yes. He allows them to make their own conclusion based on what they see and hear.

John 10 is my favorite story to illustrate this. Jesus is teaching in the temple in Jerusalem, and the teachers of the law are very frustrated and jealous of all the attention Jesus is getting. They want Jesus to claim to be the Messiah so they can accuse him of heresy. *"The Jews gathered around him, saying, 'How long will you keep us in suspense? If you are the Christ, tell us plainly.' Jesus answered, 'I did tell you, but you do not believe. The miracles I do in My Father's name speak for Me, but you do not believe because you are not My sheep. My sheep listen to My voice; I know them, and they follow Me.'"* (John 10:24-27)

People still play those kinds of games with Jesus. People make up all kinds of conditions for them to believe Jesus is the Messiah. People come up with all kinds of tests and demands; if Jesus lives up to the demands, perhaps they will believe. Put yourself in Jesus' shoes for one minute! If you were the Messiah, how would you tell people, if your goal was for them to believe and have eternal life? Too often we use authority to destroy people, we flex our muscles of authority to demonstrate our power and feed our ego. But that isn't Jesus' goal! Jesus has only one goal—for you to believe and to be saved.

WHO IS JESUS? YOUR SAVIOR FROM SIN

Ultimately, Jesus is God's anointed Messiah, who *redeems* you, not with silver or gold, but with his holy, precious blood. The Bible teaches us that sin must be atoned for. A price must be paid, a sacrifice must be offered. God's justice must be satisfied. Sin cannot be ignored. Owned and controlled by sin, we must be redeemed in order to be made righteous again. The root of life's struggles and frustrations is sin—our rebellion against God's perfection. At our deepest core, we are defensive and resentful of God's perfection and our sinfulness. We desperately want to be righteous on our own, without help from anyone. But the message of the gospel is that we are totally helpless against the power of sin and death. We need a Savior. Jesus is God's Savior for all mankind. That is the message of the Bible from beginning to end—God's story of redemption for you!

For those who believe, there is eternal life. For those who trust Jesus, and not their own righteousness, there is forgiveness, redemption, righteousness, and eternal life. The question Jesus asked Peter is still the question for every person today, "Who do you say I am?" Either Jesus is Savior and Lord, or he is something less. Who is he to you?

PERSONAL REFLECTION

1. Read over the following Bible passages several times. Reflect on the words and consider what God is saying to you through them. In the space below, write down a few notes about your thoughts.

"But when the kindness and love of God our Savior appeared, he saved us, not because of righteous things we had done, but because of his mercy. He saved us through the washing of rebirth and renewal by the Holy Spirit whom he poured out on us generously through Jesus Christ our Savior." (Titus 3:4-7)

"Here is a trustworthy saying that deserves full acceptance: Christ Jesus came into the world to save sinners—of whom I am the worst." (I Timothy 1:15)

"Jesus is the image of the invisible God, the firstborn over all creation. For by him all things were created . . . He is before all things, and in him all things hold together. And he is the head of the body, the church; he is the beginning and the firstborn from among the dead, so that in everything he might have the supremacy. For God was pleased to have all his fullness dwell in him." (Colossians 1:15-19)

2. Spend some time reflecting on how much God loves you—enough to hand over his only Son Jesus to die on the cross, so that you could be rescued from sin and death. What does it mean that Jesus is the Lord of your life? What are some of the misunderstandings you had about Jesus and the Christian faith through your life? What are some of the worries and doubts you have about life and faith?

3. Pray for God to give you his Holy Spirit of wisdom and revelation so that you might know him better.

CHAPTER 5

THE SECOND CORE TEACHING
GETTING TO KNOW JESUS THROUGH THE APOSTLES' CREED – GOD'S IDENTITY

Part III - The Holy Spirit - Your Counselor and Comforter

"**I** BELIEVE IN THE HOLY SPIRIT, the holy Christian church, the communion of saints, the forgiveness of sins, the resurrection of the body, and the life everlasting. Amen." *What does this mean? I believe that I cannot by my own reason or strength believe in Jesus Christ, my Lord, or come to him; but the Holy Spirit has called me by the gospel, enlightened me with his gifts, sanctified and kept me in the true faith. In the same way he calls, gathers, enlightens, and sanctifies the whole Christian church on earth, and keeps it with Jesus Christ in the one true faith. In this Christian church he daily and richly forgives all my sins and the sins of all believers. On the Last Day he will raise me and all the dead, and give eternal life to me and all believers in Christ. This is most certainly true.*

In my opinion, every person should go to a good Christian counselor at some point in life. Not just one or two visits, but for six months to a year of regular visits. What is the job of a good counselor? The primary job of a good counselor is to help you see and understand yourself more clearly. Too many people hope a counselor will simply confirm their preconceived portraits and characterizations of other people. Everyone likes confirmation that someone else is responsible for their problems: spouse, boss, neighbor, parent, child, or friend. The hardest thing in life is learning to be honest with yourself. It is hard for us to get an honest view of ourselves, because our eyes look out at other people. We are constantly looking at others. It is much easier to analyze the problems of other people than it is to own up to our own shortcomings. In order to see ourselves, we have to look in a mirror or listen to what someone else sees in us.

That's the Holy Spirit's job! He helps us see the reality of who we are; we are sinners in need of a Savior. The Holy Spirit opens our eyes to the reality of what God sees. He breaks down our defenses, leads us to repentance, and points us to the grace of Jesus our Savior. The Holy Spirit takes our focus away from judging other people; he wants us to get the plank out of our own eye before worrying about the speck in someone else's. The more you get to know the Holy Spirit and spend time allowing him to work on your heart through the power of God's Word, the closer you will be to God.

TWO WORKS OF THE HOLY SPIRIT

If you go to a counselor, that person has two major objectives: 1) to help you come to terms with reality; accepting responsibility for your actions; and 2) to help you make changes in your life in order to create different results. A fairly common definition of insanity is "to keep doing the same thing over and over and expect different results." That's the madness of human behavior! We don't want to change, but we want different outcomes. What we really want is for other people to change, to act more to our liking. Change really is one of the hardest things in life, because of the self-centered, sinful hearts of fallen mankind. It is one thing to come to grips with reality. It's another thing to live differently so life can be better. Real change is more than a superficial behavior. It's more than trying harder. Real change begins in the heart. When the Holy Spirit transforms our hearts, then change happens much more naturally.

The work of the Holy Spirit, the Counselor, is also twofold. 1) To work salvation; in other words, to open your eyes to the reality of your sin and your need for a Savior, creating faith in Jesus. That is the foundation of saving faith, the difference between going to heaven or hell, often referred to in the Bible as Justification. 2) To help you live differently by growing deeper in your understanding of your sin, and deeper in your grasp of God's grace, often referred to in the Bible as Sanctification or Christian living.

Too many people have a very shallow and superficial view of Christianity; they see it more as a self-help plan. They want God to help improve their lives by offering a few helpful tips. But Christianity is about a total transformation of the heart. It's about being "born again." It's about seeing the futility of a false reality where you are the center of the universe, and realizing a new reality where Jesus is the center of the universe. Through this realization, God transforms the human heart from one stubbornly defiant of God's authority to one that embraces the undeserved kindness of a holy God.

COMFORTER

All human beings are naturally defensive about digging deep into their hearts and uncovering past failures, sins, and pains. Personal fears, failures, insecurities, and pain, can cause people to put up incredibly strong resistance. When you set out to help a person get to the bottom of the truth about who they are, you risk a lot. You risk resentment, anger, hatred, and maybe the end of a relationship. That's why counseling must be done with a deep sense of love and kindness. The person receiving counsel must know that the counselor loves them. They must feel safe sharing their deepest feelings. A good counselor must be a great comforter. That's quite a combination for a good counselor: finding the courage to tell the truth, the wisdom to ask tough questions, and the tenderness and compassion to comfort and love unconditionally.

That's the Holy Spirit—our Counselor and Comforter! The Holy Spirit is the Spirit of Jesus, the perfect combination of truth and grace. Read through the gospels and see why people were so attracted to Jesus! Jesus had no hidden agenda. He wasn't out to hurt anyone. He told the truth with brutal honesty, and yet his kindness and compassion were evident to everyone. The Holy Spirit wants to bring you into fellowship with your Creator God—Father, Son, and Holy Spirit. In that fellowship is the greatest peace a person can ever find: a God who loves you too much to leave you in the false reality of sin.

CHRISTIAN DENOMINATIONS

This is a side note regarding the theology of the Holy Spirit. Many of the distinctions that exist between different Christian denominations exist because of their interpretations of Scripture regarding the work of the Holy Spirit. When is a person "saved?" Does a person play a part in the process of conversion? How does the Holy Spirit bring a person to saving faith? How does the Holy Spirit use the sacraments (baptism and the Lord's Supper) to work in a person's heart? How much is human will a part of spiritual transformation? How a church answers these questions will inevitably affect the way they carry out their ministry. If you have been a part of different Christian churches, you may have noticed that they have different practices, different cultures, different points of emphasis, and different personalities. Those different practices are not the result of arbitrary decisions, but rather, an outgrowth of deeply held beliefs about how the Holy Spirit works. If you hold a certain belief about how the Holy Spirit creates and strengthens faith, you will build your church and ministry around those practices. Part of this chapter is intended to help clarify some of the differences between Christian denominations.

HUMAN WILL VS. HOLY SPIRIT'S POWER

Basically, there are three different views on how the Holy Spirit works within Protestant Christianity. Please pardon my use of some rather rare theological terms to explain these concepts. They are not intended to give you a seminary level course in Holy Spirit theology, but to have some sense of why different Christian denominations have different practices in ministry.

The first view is called Synergism, and it has its roots in Arminius and Zwingli (two theologians from the Reformation.) This view is held by many Baptist, Non-denominational, and Pentecostal churches. It is occasionally referred to as "decision theology." Synergy means working together, and it proposes that the Holy Spirit works on the human heart, but once the truth of the Bible has been presented, a person has the free will to decide whether to accept or reject Jesus. A church that holds to synergistic theology will place a strong emphasis in their ministry on asking people to make the decision to become a Christian, to participate in an altar call and pray a believer's prayer. They place a strong emphasis on knowing when a person made the decision to become a Christian and almost always believe in adult immersion baptism as a symbolic and public profession of faith. This teaching leads to some challenging questions about infant baptism and the age of accountability, which will be addressed in chapter 7.

The second teaching is referred to as Monergism. This word means "one work" and holds that the human will has no role in conversion, that it is completely the work of the Holy Spirit. This teaching has its roots in the theology of John Calvin. This theology is more common in churches which are Presbyterian, Methodist, or Anglican. In these churches, you won't hear the emphasis on making a decision to accept Jesus. Instead you will hear strong proclamation of law to bring people to repentance, and strong proclamation of the gospel to bring people to faith. But the response of the hearer will not receive as much emphasis as the redeeming work of Jesus. This teaching is often referred to as "double predestination."

The third teaching is held by the Lutheran Church and can be referred to as Limited Free Will. It is more closely related to Monergism. Martin Luther wrote, "I cannot by my own reason or strength, believe in Jesus Christ my Lord or come to him." That is monergistic, only the work of the Holy Spirit. But, Lutherans hold that people do have the free will to reject God. To many people this seems like a paradox, a conflict, which it is! If I have the free will to reject God, isn't that the same as the free will to accept him? It sounds logical, but that is not what the Bible says. The Bible says God chooses us, but we have the ability to reject Jesus. If you are saved, it is only by God's grace. If you are damned, it is your fault. That doesn't sound fair. And that's the paradox of grace; it isn't fair! God's kingdom doesn't work on fairness. If it did, all people would deserve only hell. God's kingdom is based on grace—which is a mystery to sinful mankind. The result is that Lutherans practice ministry which does not emphasize a decision, strongly proclaims law and gospel, and baptizes infants.

EMPHASIS AND BALANCE

Doctrinal differences between Christian churches are often a matter of different emphases, rather than a complete dismissal or approval of a particular teaching. After many years of teaching and talking to people from different Christian denominations, here are the major differences I have observed in emphasis.

- *Catholic Church* – Emphasizes incomplete salvation and the need for good works. Christ died to save sinners, but good works are needed to complete the goal.

- *Lutheran Church* – Emphasizes forgiven sinners; a life of growing in deeper knowledge of sin and repentance, and deepening knowledge of God's grace in the gospel.

- *Evangelical Reformed/ Protestants* – Emphasizes obedient servant. Once a person has decided to accept Jesus and has been saved by the gospel, the primary need is obedience to the teachings of Jesus.

These matters of balance and emphasis create a very different culture from church to church. And they are deeply rooted in the theology of the Holy Spirit and his work.

THE CONNECTOR

If I had to pick one word that describes the work of the Holy Spirit, it would be the word connector. God the Father created all things. Jesus completed the redeeming work of God. And the Holy Spirit connects people to their Creator and Redeemer. How does the Holy Spirit create that connection? He does it through "means." In the Bible, God tells us that the Holy Spirit bridges the gap between a holy God and sinful people through God's Word and the Sacraments. Those are the connection points. The Holy Spirit penetrates into our hearts through those means. If those are the means God promises us the Holy Spirit is working through, you can understand that they are central to the life of a Church, and the life of a Christian.

I like to use the analogy of a person who receives an inheritance from a rich uncle who lives overseas. The uncle dies and the money is there for the taking. Although it has been given, it must be received somehow: travel overseas to get it, set up a wire transfer, receive a check, or any other option that works. The same reality holds for God's grace. Jesus died on the cross for the sins of all people. But not all will be saved. God gives that forgiveness through the Holy Spirit working through the means of God's Word, baptism, and the Lord's Supper. The Bible has occasional examples of the Holy Spirit working through different means: dreams, visions, and audible voices. And it is certainly possible for God to work however he chooses. But the Bible promises that the Holy Spirit works to bring faith, forgiveness, and spiritual life through the means of grace: God's Word, baptism and the Lord's Supper. And so we cling to those promises and keep those means central in the life of the Church.

PERSONAL CONNECTION

While the church is a critical part of God's work on earth, at the end of the day Christianity is about a personal relationship with God. In a very personal way, God invites you to be in relationship with him; Father, Son, and Holy Spirit. Christian author C.S. Lewis describes a relationship with God as a dance of fellowship. The Father, Son, and Holy Spirit are constantly glorifying each other, eternally perpetuating love and life. Through the work of the Holy Spirit, you are invited into that eternal dance of fellowship. God wants to speak directly into your life. He doesn't want to be connected to you indirectly, through your relationship with someone else who is close to God. He wants to connect directly to you. He wants you to know him, to know his Word, to listen to his voice, to talk to him, to enjoy his presence. That happens as you are personally connected to God— through worship, prayer, Bible study, devotions, and quiet time to meditate and listen to God's voice.

I think the most essential practice for every Christian is to spend time every day in what I call devotional meditation; reading Bible passages, maybe a devotion, meditating on that word, listening to God's voice, praying, and reflecting on what God is teaching you. The Holy Spirit is God's counselor and comforter. Be sure to set a daily appointment.

PERSONAL REFLECTION

1. Read over the following Bible passages several times. Reflect on the words and consider what God is saying to you through them. In the space below, write down a few notes about your thoughts.

Jesus said, "But the Counselor, the Holy Spirit, whom the Father will send in My name, will teach you all things and will remind you of everything I have said to you. Peace I leave with you; My peace I give you. I do not give to you as the world gives. Do not let your hearts be troubled and do not be afraid." (John 14:26-27)

"But the fruit of the Spirit is love, joy, peace, patience, kindness, goodness, faithfulness, gentleness, and self-control. Against such things there is no law." (Galatians 5:22-23)

"O Lord, You have searched me and You know me. You know when I sit and when I rise; You perceive my thoughts from afar. For You created my inmost being; You knit me together in my mother's womb. I praise You because I am fearfully and wonderfully made; Your works are wonderful, I know that full well." (Psalm 139:1-2, 13-14)

2. Think about some of the deep secrets you hide in your heart; people who have hurt you deeply in the past, people you can't forgive, things you wish you had never done. Ask the Holy Spirit to help you be honest about your own sins, to help you forgive those who have hurt you. Ask God what things lie deep in your heart. Ask God to open up your heart so you can lay them before him for healing, forgiveness, and a fresh start. Ask God to help you be honest with yourself, and with him.

3. Pray for God to give you his Holy Spirit of wisdom and revelation so that you might know him better.

CHAPTER 6

THE THIRD CORE TEACHING
GETTING TO KNOW JESUS THROUGH THE LORD'S PRAYER

Communicating with God

WHY PRAYER? PERSONALIZING YOUR FAITH

ONE OF THE BIGGEST OBSTACLES for Christians is to personalize their faith. After all, the Bible is a book about other people who lived thousands of years ago. In one way, the Bible is very impersonal because it is about God relating to people in history. But God's intention is that the Bible would be very personal. One of my favorite sayings is, "The Bible is not a book about what God *did*, but about what God *does*." Think about that for a minute! The same ways in which God was active throughout the history of the world are the same ways that God is active today. And the same ways that God communicated with people in the Bible are the ways He is communicating with you today.

Prayer is one of the greatest gifts God has given to us to help personalize our faith. God really wants to have a personal dialogue with you. God wants your life to be an ongoing dialogue and interaction. Prayer is a big part of that dialogue. The other parts of a personal dialogue with God are: 1) meditating on God's Word; and 2) applying God's Word to your life.

This process of personalizing the Christian faith can be referred to as "devotions." Devotions: the process of growing in devotion to Jesus. Being devoted to someone means spending time to listen, understand, and act accordingly. A personal devotional life for a Christian includes listening to Jesus, seeking to understand the Word of God, and acting accordingly.

Martin Luther used three Latin words to describe the process of personal devotions: oratio (prayer), meditatio (meditation), and tentatio (struggle). He described the process as asking God to give you his Holy Spirit so you can understand his Word, meditating on God's Word, and struggling as you apply it to your life. Too often Christians have a very limited understanding of prayer, seeing it only as asking God for the things they want. Think about that for a minute! What if the only conversation you ever had with other people was telling them the things you want from them? My guess is that you wouldn't have very many friends or any close relationships. In deep and meaningful relationships, communication is the holistic practice of listening, seeking to understand the other person, responding in truth and love, and also sharing your own thoughts and needs.

Martin Luther had another great saying about prayer. He said that when he had a day with too many things to accomplish, he would spend an extra hour in prayer. I would like to make a suggestion without being legalistic. Try to spend at least 15-20 minutes every day meditating on God's Word, praying, and writing down some notes on your thoughts and prayers. The thoughts and prayers you write down should have to do with your daily life, on your successes and failures of applying God's Word to your life. Sports teams spend long hours every week looking at game film to evaluate and improve their performance. It's not easy watching your mistakes, but it can be a great source for improvement. So it is with the Christian life! It's not easy examining your life in light of God's Word. It shouldn't be hard to find many areas where you do not live up to God's expectations. As you grow in your knowledge of God's Word, you will grow in your understanding of God's heart, and in your knowledge of God's ways. You will grow in your ability to identify sinful desires and thoughts and in your ability to repent deeply and genuinely. And most of all, you will grow in your amazement of God's grace. You will marvel at his unconditional love. You will hear and recognize God's voice drowning out the voice of Satan and the world trying to lead you astray. And, you will know God and his heart.

WHAT IS PRAYER?

Very simply, prayer is communicating with God. Prayer is often intimidating to people, especially praying out loud and praying with other people. And that is perfectly understandable. When you meet a new person, the conversation is often rather uncomfortable and superficial. Communication that is deep and sincere is dependent on a strong relationship that takes time to develop. So don't be intimidated by prayer! Take your time.

Prayer is also approaching God, which can only be done through Jesus Christ. Prayer might be one of the most misunderstood spiritual activities. When it comes to spiritual activities, attending church and reading the Bible are often neglected. But most people say they pray. Maybe that's because prayer seems to be a much easier spiritual activity—it costs nothing, no sacrifice, no time out of your schedule, no commitment. At least it seems that way. The truth is, no sinner has a right to talk to the Holy God who created the universe. There was a tremendous sacrifice that was paid for sinners to approach a holy God – Jesus laid down his life to tear down that barrier. And faith in Jesus Christ is the only means to approach God.

In America, where the government is "of the people, by the people, for the people" there is little understanding of what it is like to be governed by a king. Americans have a tough time relating to the Biblical concept of a king. In a monarchy, the king has absolute authority. With one word, a person can be sentenced to death. No one approaches the king without an invitation. A king must have an almost ruthless heart at times to guard against evildoers. God is the Almighty King of the universe. No sinner has any right to call on his name. No sinner is entitled to offer his or her petitions to the king. The only way into the king's presence is to be one with the king's Son—Jesus.

Many people are misguided about prayer. Many people think every petition to some higher power is heard and acknowledged. Nothing could be further from the truth. The teaching called universalism has overtaken American culture—the belief that all religions lead to the same God. Most religions have a conservative and a liberal branch. The conservatives in most religions believe that their version of God is the only true God. And the liberal branches hold that all paths lead to the same God.

If you take the Bible to be the inspired, inerrant Word of God—and the only source of truth about the one true God—then universalism is a difficult option. The only way to the Father is through the redeeming work of his Son Jesus. And the only way to approach his throne in prayer is through the forgiveness of sins that comes through faith in Jesus. To those who live in that relationship, prayer becomes the path to a genuine relationship with the God who created you and redeemed you.

HOW DO I PRAY?

If you have ever asked this question, you are in good company. The 12 disciples of Jesus had the same request, "Jesus, teach us to pray." The Bible reveals that Jesus often went off to quiet places by himself to pray. He prayed all night before choosing his disciples. The disciples saw Jesus taking time to pray and somehow knew that they should do the same. The response of Jesus was to give them, and us, the Lord's Prayer. The Lord's Prayer is both a prayer to be spoken, and also a model for a rich, full, and mature prayer life. Essentially, Jesus reveals the seven topics that every Christian should include in their conversations with God. In *Luther's Small Catechism*, they are called the seven petitions.

Introduction - Our Father who art in heaven

The first thing Jesus teaches us about prayer is how to approach God, the same way a person approaches a loving father—with respect, joy, and peace. God is not a far away, impersonal, harsh authoritarian. He is a king; but he is a loving and kind king.

First Petition - Hallowed be Thy Name

The first topic God wants us to consider is his holiness. God's name is set apart from all other names on earth: Yahweh, Jesus, and Counselor. He alone is perfect, without sin. He is the judge and ruler of all creation. His name is holy. The only question is, "Is his name holy in my heart?" We are asking God to make his name holy in our hearts. You can pray and meditate at length on this concept. The Scriptures are filled with passages about God's holiness.

Second Petition - Thy Kingdom Come

God wants us to be focused on his kingdom! If you want to meditate on God's kingdom, read the parables of Jesus in the gospels (Matthew, Mark, Luke, and John). Jesus often introduced his parables with the words, "The kingdom of God is like . . . " God's kingdom works differently than the world. God's kingdom works on grace—which is a foreign concept to sinful people. Ask God to help you understand the ways of his kingdom, and to live in that reality—to conform your life to it!

Third Petition - Thy Will be done on earth as it is in heaven

Is your life dictated by accomplishing your agenda, or is it driven and motivated by carrying out God's will? God's mission is to save sinners, to reveal his truth and grace, to love and care for people. Every aspect of your life is a calling from God to help carry out his kingdom's work. Living in that reality is a totally different existence than living to accomplish your agenda. Meditate on God's will for your life and ask the Holy Spirit to keep your heart and mind focused on his will.

Fourth Petition - Give us this day our daily bread

If you didn't notice, the first three petitions are focused on God; his identity, his kingdom, and his will. The next four petitions focus more on your daily life. They begin with your physical needs. God knows we have physical needs, but he wants us to keep that in perspective. Daily bread is a secondary need. Although we need daily bread—food, drink, shelter, supplies, and more— that need should remind us of our dependence on God. It should remind us that everything we have is a gift from God. It should remind us to live by faith, trusting that God will provide our daily needs. It should remind us to be generous with our abundance of possessions. Why stockpile supplies and money if God promises to meet our daily needs? Meditate on where physical needs fit into your heart and life. Ask the Holy Spirit to give you the right perspective.

Fifth Petition – And forgive us our sins, as we forgive those who sin against us

It's hard to function without daily bread, so God takes care of that concern first. But the greatest concern in life is really sin. The issue of sin has eternal consequences! If sin is not dealt with, it could mean an eternity in hell. God knows the importance of repentance and forgiveness. Every day a Christian should reflect deeply on his thoughts, words, and actions—to confess deeply and sincerely, and to receive Christ's forgiveness. Spend time meditating on the Ten Commandments. Read and pray Psalms of repentance such as Psalm 32, 51, and 139.

And then deal with the other side of sin, forgiving those who sin against you! The two greatest spiritual dangers are: 1) intentional, unrepentant sin; and, 2) the unwillingness to forgive others. In Psalm 19, King David prays for God to "keep your servant from willful sins, may they not rule over me." David understood the incredible spiritual danger of a hardened heart, calloused to the truth of sin (Psalm 32:3-5). An unwillingness to forgive other people has the same effect; it hardens our hearts (Matthew 18:21-35). It's not easy to forgive people who sin against you. But holding people hostage is no way to live—it drains the life out of us and also out of others. There is a saying about unforgiveness and resentment: "It is like drinking poison and hoping the other person will die." Don't let resentment poison your soul.

Sixth Petition – Lead us not into temptation

Sinful human beings are easily deceived by Satan. And that is the way Satan usually operates. He doesn't present the honest reality of good and evil, and then ask us to make an educated decision. He intentionally misleads us with promises of contentment, gratification, pleasure, and success. But his true motive is to lead us away from God and destroy us. That's why the Bible often compares us to sheep, easily led astray, and defenseless. Peter reminds us, *"Be self-controlled and alert. Your enemy the devil prowls around like a roaring lion looking for someone to devour" (I Peter 5:8).* Meditating on this topic can be a constant reminder that life is full of temptations that can lead us away from God. Ask the Holy Spirit to open your eyes to those temptations and to give you strength to resist.

Seventh petition – Deliver us from evil

This prayer reminds us how powerless we really are against sin, Satan, and death. This battle is stronger than our own willpower. No matter how hard you try not to sin, to avoid temptation, and to overcome Satan—you don't have the power. *"Not by might, not by power, but by My Spirit, says the Lord." (Zechariah 4:6)* We need God's Holy Spirit. We need his power. We need more than help or advice. We need to be connected to God's power. Don't be deceived! You cannot overcome evil by trying harder. The only option to overcome evil is to be united with God's Holy Spirit through faith in Jesus

Christ. Pray for God to fill you with his Holy Spirit! Ask God to give you his strength!

LET'S PRAY

I don't remember who told me this, but it sure made sense: "He who doesn't pray in regular times and regular places, probably doesn't pray at all." It's important to have a balance of scheduled routine and spontaneous impulse. Most married couples work at keeping that balance. If you don't schedule time together, it may not happen at all. Of course there are always unexpected times to communicate, which is great. Here are a few suggestions to consider regarding your prayer life. But be sure to establish routines that work well for you. Don't feel pressured into legalistic rules.

Pray before meals. Some people say the same prayers before and after meals as a family. Other families ask one person to make up a prayer. For most people, you stop three times a day to eat a meal. It is a good reminder of the words Jesus quoted from the Old Testament, *"Man does not live on bread alone, but on every word that comes from the mouth of God." (Matthew 4:4)* Meals are a great time to remember that everything is a gift from God.

Pray in the morning. Many people use the morning to have a devotion and prayer. You can use a devotion book, read portions of the Bible, and pray. It's a great way to start the day focused on walking with Jesus.

Pray before you go to bed. It's a great time to think through the day and consider God's blessings.

Pray with your children. Nothing will help them realize God's presence more than praying with you.

Pray with your spouse. It's hard to be angry and hold a grudge while you are praying. Prayer has a way of breaking down petty arguments.

Pray with your Christian friends. You will be surprised how receptive people are to having you pray for them out loud while you are together. In my entire life, I've never had anyone turn me down. You don't need to be a pastor to pray with someone! Trust me, the other person is not worried about theological perfection or poetic phrasing. What they crave is God's power and peace—and prayer can give that!

Pray with people who may not be Christians. I know this one is a little more sensitive, and in today's politically correct world, you may need to use extra caution. But if people are willing to share their concerns with you, ask them if you can pray for them. You might be surprised how open they might be.

Use printed prayers. My grandfather gave me a book printed by Concordia Publishing House titled, *My Prayer Book*. It contains beautiful prayers, one for every morning and evening of the month, and then a multitude of topical prayers for different spiritual or life issues. Sometimes you might find yourself praying for the same things, with the same words all the time. A prayer book can expand and deepen your prayer life.

Don't forget, praying is a whole lot more than asking God for stuff you want. It's a critical part of a dialogue between you and your God! His Word is very personal for you, and your prayers are very personal for him! Don't be afraid to engage and grow into a deep and meaningful prayer life with God.

PERSONAL REFLECTION

1. Read over the following Bible passages several times. Reflect on the words and consider what God is saying to you through them. In the space below, write down a few notes about your thoughts.

    Jesus said, "Come to Me, all you who are weary and burdened, and I will give you rest. Take My yoke upon you and learn from Me, for I am gentle and humble in heart, and you will find rest for your souls. For My yoke is easy and My burden is light." (Matthew 11:28-30)

Jesus said, "And when you pray, do not be like the hypocrites, for they love to pray standing in the synagogues and on the street corners to be seen by men. I tell you the truth, they have received their reward in full. But when you pray, go into your room, close the door and pray to your Father, who is unseen. Then your Father, who sees what is done in secret, will reward you." (Matthew 6:5)

"Be joyful always; pray continually; give thanks in all circumstances, for this is God's will for you in Christ Jesus." (I Thessalonians 5:16-18)

2. Give some thought to your prayer life. What is the most meaningful place and time for you to pray? Do you pray with your family—both children and spouse? How can you begin to have a more active prayer life? Is there someone you know who can help you? Make it easy; read a couple of verses in the Bible, and have a short prayer about what the verses say.

3. Pray for God to give you his Holy Spirit of wisdom and revelation so that you might know him better.

CHAPTER 7

THE FOURTH CORE TEACHING
GETTING TO KNOW JESUS THROUGH BAPTISM

Being Identified with and Connected to God

MEANS OF GRACE

A GOOD FRIEND IS ONE WHO LISTENS, takes time to know you, your strengths, your preferred ways of receiving affirmation and love, and your weaknesses. A good friend thoughtfully takes into account the best ways to communicate and relate with you. A good friend has in mind the goal to bless you and help you, not work against you. That kind of attitude is kind, gracious, loving, and helpful. That kind of attitude draws a person out, creates trust, and builds relationship. An awareness of the best ways to connect with another person is important.

The same is true with the way God's Holy Spirit connects with us. God knows we need things that are tangible, defined, and concrete in order to build trust. He knows we struggle with things that are abstract and vague. Relationships can be very vague—and fragile! But God has chosen several ways to connect with us in order to make our relationship with him concrete, clear, and defined. Those ways are referred to as the "means of grace," and through these means, God promises that his Holy Spirit will deliver grace to us. There are three ways that God connects to us in clear, defined ways: 1) through the Word of God; 2) through baptism; and 3) through the Lord's Supper. The Holy Spirit works through the Word of God as it is read, studied, preached, taught, memorized, and pondered. Baptism and the Lord's Supper are referred to as "sacraments." The word sacrament literally means a sacred act and involves physical objects: water, bread, and wine. Through these three means, the Holy Spirit connects us to God by creating and strengthening our faith, forgiving our sins, and dwelling in us.

The Holy Spirit is like the wind. He moves as he pleases, and he is beyond anyone's ability to control. God can work any way he chooses. But he promises to work, to connect with us, to give us his grace through these special means. And because of God's promise to work through these means, they are the primary focus of Christian worship and ministry. They should be central in the life of every Christian and every Christian Church. Prayer, praise, singing, service, fellowship, and other Christian practices are also important! But since God promises to create faith, forgive sins, change hearts, and transform lives through a specific means, we grasp firmly to those promises. He has given us these spiritual gifts, so we can be confident of his unshakable love for us!

BAPTISM AND ENGAGEMENT

Because relationships can be so fragile, people living in community create cultural standards that help reinforce commitment. Governments create laws to strengthen certain relationships in marriage, parenting, and business, and relating to positions of authority and power. Those laws impose punishments on people who break commitments and promises. In effect, people are collectively agreeing that commitment to relationships is so important for a strong community that laws are needed to help strengthen them. It is not socially acceptable to make promises and to recklessly break them. Lives can be destroyed by broken promises.

The government has clear laws about marriage. In America, there really aren't laws regarding engagement. But there are certainly societal standards, unwritten rules that are in place regarding an engagement for marriage. And quite often, unwritten codes of conduct which are enforced through social pressure can be more powerful than any written rule. In the process of getting engaged in our culture, a man traditionally buys a rather expensive engagement ring and asks a woman to marry him. The ring is given as a visible sign, signaling other men to stay away, and holding the couple to a deeper level of commitment. Public announcements are made to family and friends. Often, an announcement and engagement picture are published in the newspaper. Announcing something publicly has a way of deepening commitment. Break that commitment, and there will be repercussions. Break that commitment maliciously or cruelly and your name may be tarnished significantly. It simply isn't socially acceptable to make that promise and not take it seriously. The promise is made so the relationship can continue to deepen and move toward marriage with confidence.

With this promise, plans are made for two people to begin a new life together. Plans are made to merge two households into one. It would be very risky for a person to start planning without a firm, public commitment. But in addition to public commitment, it is vital for both people to open their hearts even deeper and increase their commitment to one another.

Similar to engagement, God promises to be our God and we to be his people through baptism. He seals his commitment to us as he creates faith in Jesus in infants and strengthens saving faith in older children and adults. Through baptism, Christ commits himself to his bride, the Church (you and me) as our beloved, divine Bridegroom!

Baptism is a sacrament

A sacrament is simply defined as a sacred act. But in most churches, it also refers to specific ceremonies. In the Lutheran Church, a sacrament is defined by three things:

1. Commanded and instituted by Jesus

2. Combines the Word of God with a physical element

3. Imparts the forgiveness of sins

One of the reasons a sacrament is such a blessing is the connection between something intangible and invisible to something tangible. In baptism, God connects faith and forgiveness to water and the Word of God.

Quite often people misunderstand God's primary intention in baptism. It is not an arbitrary ceremony that God demands of us because he likes to impose obligations on people. God gives us baptism as a gift, a means through which he gives his saving grace to us. We receive faith in Jesus, complete forgiveness, the guarantee of heaven, and a physical verification of his great love and commitment to us! God gives baptism to bless us! He knows that we are physical beings who have a strong dependence on physical affirmation. When things are more concrete our hearts rest easy. For example, if you buy a house from someone, it is exciting to reach a verbal agreement and shake hands on a deal. But having the title to the property in your hands brings even more assurance that it really does belong to you.

The same is true for saving faith. It's great to know that Jesus died for your sins, forgives you and loves you unconditionally. But it sure helps to know that through baptism those promises are assured. And that's what baptism does! Through water and the Word of God, the Holy Spirit acts, sins are forgiven, and faith is imparted. Ultimately, our hope is in Jesus Christ our Savior, not in the act of baptism. But God gives us the gift of baptism to create, strengthen and deepen our connection to Jesus.

In the Old Testament, the Israelites had a ritual called ceremonial washing. It was a physical reminder of a spiritual reality—a person is made unclean with sin. Sin needs to be washed away so a person can enter the presence of God. Martin Luther once said that every morning when you wash your face, remember your baptism, that your sins have been washed away.

Baptismal assurance

In the Bible, St. Paul wrote in Romans 6 that we are baptized into the death and resurrection of Jesus. Through baptism we are connected to the redeeming work of Jesus. His crucifixion satisfies God's demands of justice for us. His resurrection gives us victory over death. Through baptism our sins are washed away and we are new creations in Jesus.

In any relationship there are good days and bad days. When you fight or argue with someone you love, it's hard not to have doubts about the relationship. You worry if the person you love will stop loving you. What if my friend, spouse, or child walks away from me? The fear of a broken relationship can be devastating. It's no way to live! That is the last thing God wants. As a Christian, you will have bad days when sin gets the best of you. You might have a bad week, month, or year! But God never wants you to doubt his love for you. He doesn't want sin to rule over you, nor does he want you to fall into despair. He wants you to live in his grace—repentant of your sins, and grateful for his grace.

Infant Baptism

Probably the most visible difference between certain Christian denominations is their practice regarding infant baptism. Some churches baptize infants; others do not. Which one is right? If both sides of this issue were honest, they would admit it is a challenging question. Nowhere in the Bible does it explicitly say to "baptize infants." And nowhere in the Bible does it say "don't baptize infants." If the Bible doesn't say specifically one way or the other, how do we know what to do? The answer is: you reach a conclusion based on the best information the Bible offers.

Here's the simplest guideline I can offer. Most churches that believe in "decision theology" (remember Chapter 5?) don't practice infant baptism. They believe that faith comes through intellectual comprehension of the gospel and a free will decision to believe in Jesus as Savior and Lord. Baptism follows that decision as a public witness of faith. There are two teachings that are closely associated with this view of baptism. First, it is connected with the teaching called "once saved, always saved." In other words, once a person makes a genuine and sincere decision to be a Christian, they cannot fall away from that faith. And secondly, it is connected with the teaching called "the age of accountability." In other words, a child is not held accountable for his sins until he reaches an age where he can understand the concept of sin. Although that age varies for individuals, it is generally considered to be around the age of twelve.

Churches that believe in no free will, or limited free will, tend to practice infant baptism. If you remember the chapter on the Holy Spirit, Martin Luther explained, "I cannot by my own reason or strength believe in Jesus Christ my Lord or come to him." Since reason and free will are not a part of coming to faith, baptism is a miraculous way of imparting saving faith to those who are not old enough to process the gospel intellectually. Hearing the gospel and having the Holy Spirit work through your intellect is certainly one way of coming to saving faith. But it is still the power of the Holy Spirit overpowering a person's will, not a person's free will. Churches that practice infant baptism have two closely connected teachings and practices. First, these churches often hold that the Bible teaches a person can fall away from their faith. A person can reject God and his grace. Second, these churches usually have a practice called "confirmation." At an age when children can more fully learn the fundamental teachings of Christianity, they are taught. At the end of the instruction, they are offered the opportunity to confirm the faith they received in baptism—and to pledge their faithfulness in following Jesus.

The challenge

At the end of the line, both sides of this issue have a challenging question to answer about the origin of faith. Those who hold to the teaching of total free will—decision theology—will be challenged if a person who was once a Christian completely rejects Jesus. The explanation offered is that their "conversion" was not genuine and sincere in the first place. In other words, they were never truly converted. The challenge in that answer is the constant uncertainty of a person wondering if their conversion was genuine. This is particularly difficult when struggling with a particular sin. A person begins to wonder, "If I really love Jesus, why do I struggle with this particular sin? Maybe I need to be converted again." That focus constantly leads a person to look inward, which is a very hopeless exercise, because every person is filled with sin. And that mindset can lead to many conversion experiences, because hope can only rest on your own genuineness. The second challenge is defending the teaching of "the age of accountability" from the Bible. The Bible does not have much to say about God not holding children accountable for sin. In fact, it says quite the opposite! Consider these Scripture passages:

"Surely I was sinful at birth, sinful from the time my mother conceived me." *(Psalm 51:5)*

"Even from birth the wicked go astray; from the womb they are wayward and speak lies." *(Psalm 58:3)*

Those churches that practice infant baptism have some challenging questions as well. First of all, if an infant is baptized, at what point is saving faith lost as a child matures? What if that baptismal faith is not nurtured? What happens if that child is not instructed about the Savior's love? When does that baptismal faith no longer save because there is no knowledge of the gospel? Those are tough questions! It is vitally important for parents to continually give their children the admonition of the law and the nurture of the gospel in order for baptismal faith to be kept alive (Proverbs 22:6). Spirit-created faith must also be Spirit-fed in order to survive and thrive!

Another challenging question is what happens to an infant who dies before being baptized? The answer to that question is: God's grace is not limited by baptism. We don't have a clear answer to all of the questions about baptism, but we do have clear answers about God's grace and mercy.

Mystery

Finally, every Christian must admit that there is a mystery that can only be known by God. The great mystery of the cross is, "Why are some saved and others not?" Quite simply, that question is the theological end of the road. We cannot know the mind of God, but we can know the heart of God. Finally, Christianity is based on faith and trust, not logic and reason. Don't get me wrong, the Bible is very logical, and reason is a gift of God that Christians should embrace. But the life of a Christian is a lot like a child. A child simply cannot understand what his parents do. At some point a child must trust that his parents love him and have his best interests at heart.

Relationships are the essence of life. They are a journey, an adventure; they are new and fresh every day. Relationships are not just a part of life; they are life. It begins with living in relationship with God—your Creator and Redeemer. And it flows over into the relationships with your neighbors and friends. It is God's great desire that you have great confidence in him! His love is perfect. He will never leave you or abandon you. The greatest fears you have in human relationships can never be realized in your relationship with God. Knowing that you are secure in his love gives you the strength to step out and take the risk of loving others the way he loves you.

Baptism is a great gift from God to assure you of his love. Don't overthink it! Don't get trapped in trying to figure out the mystery of it, or the unknowns. Take it for what God intended it to be: a clear, tangible means of receiving his grace.

PERSONAL REFLECTION

1. Read over the following Bible passages several times. Reflect on the words and consider what God is saying to you through them. In the space below, write down a few notes about your thoughts.

"Don't you know that all of us who were baptized into Christ Jesus were baptized into his death? We were therefore buried with him through baptism into death in order that, just as Christ was raised from the dead through the glory of the Father, we too may live a new life. If we have been united with him like this in his death, we will certainly also be united with him in his resurrection." (Romans 6:3-5)

"When the people heard this (the gospel), they were cut to the heart and said to Peter and the other apostles, "Brothers, what shall we do?" Peter replied, "Repent and be baptized, every one of you, in the name of Jesus Christ for the forgiveness of sin. And you will receive the gift of the Holy Spirit. The promise is for you and your children and for all who are far off—for all whom the Lord our God will call." (Acts 2:37-39)

"But when the kindness and love of God our Savior appeared, He saved us, not because of righteous things we had done, but because of his mercy. He saved us through the washing of rebirth and renewal by the Holy Spirit, whom he poured out on us generously through Jesus Christ our Savior, so that, having been justified by his grace, we might become heirs having the hope of eternal life." (Titus 3:4-7)

2. Do you struggle with spiritual pride (I'm a good enough person) or with spiritual inadequacy (my sins are too bad for God to love me)? How can God's gift of baptism help you with that? If you are married, think of how special your wedding ring is—a constant reminder of your commitment and love. Think of baptism as the same mark of God's love for you.

3. Pray for God to give you his Holy Spirit of wisdom and revelation so that you might know him better.

CHAPTER 8

THE FIFTH CORE TEACHING
GETTING TO KNOW JESUS THROUGH CONFESSION AND FORGIVENESS

Genuine Repentance, Amazing Grace

*"If we claim to be without sin, we deceive ourselves and the truth is not in us.
If we confess our sin, he is faithful and just and will forgive us our sins and
purify us from all unrighteousness. If we claim we have not sinned, we make
him out to be a liar and his word has no place in our lives." (I John 1:8-10)*

THOSE WORDS ARE CRITICALLY IMPORTANT to understanding
the essence of Christianity. Sin is the obstacle to intimacy with God.
And every human being is by nature sinful. In spite of that truth, the
hardest thing for any human being to do is accept responsibility for sin.
Jesus called Satan the "father of lies," and the "master of deception." Satan's
number one tactic is to convince people that sin is really not sin. Satan gets
people to question and defy God's authority—which is easily done, because
our sinfulness naturally makes us rebellious against authority. The denial of
sin ultimately makes life unsatisfying and miserable. And yet we do it all
the time.

You cannot overestimate the importance of true repentance in the life of a Christian. When we are not repentant, we make God out to be a liar! Billy Graham said that the secret to a good marriage is having two good forgivers. How true! The same is true for any relationship— repentance and forgiveness is essential.

THE PSYCHOLOGY OF SIN

Many people think of sin far too simplistically, an action that is mean or cruel. Sin is so much deeper and more complicated. It has to do with our thoughts, motives, and heart. Sin also has to do with the good things we ought to do, but don't. The root of sin lies deep in our psyche, our rationalizations, and motives. We become masters of putting on a front to make it look like our actions are motivated by selflessness, kindness, and love. But deep down inside, most of our actions are motivated by selfishness—manipulating life to get what we want for ourselves. If we are honest with ourselves, most of what we do is self-serving.

The gospel is really the only power on earth to open up a human heart to face the reality of how ugly sin really is. Only when a person is deeply secure in the unconditional love and grace of God, knowing that he is absolutely accepted because of the saving work of Jesus, will he ever be able to be honest about sin. The deeper grasp a person has of the gospel, the stronger he will grow at admitting sin and giving other people the benefit of grace.

People who view themselves as religious and moral have a tendency to justify the sins of the heart that have to do with motive. The human tendency is to harshly judge overt immoral behavior like stealing, murder, violence, and other crimes, but to minimize sins of the heart like greed, hatred, or selfishness. The Bible exposes that kind of self-righteous thinking that Jesus condemns so clearly.

It is often easier to witness to people who are openly irreligious. People who don't view themselves as moral, religious, and god-fearing often have a sense that what they are doing is somehow wrong in God's eyes. But they are often caught up in a life of crime or immorality because it is the only life they have ever seen or experienced. It's hard for them to imagine any other way of life. That's why Jesus loved to hang around the openly irreligious—tax collectors, prostitutes, and outcasts. They were more open to the presence and love of Jesus. The people Jesus had the strongest rebukes for were the self-righteous, the unrepentant, and the morally and spiritually proud.

The gospel radically reframes spirituality. Instead of God being concerned about good and bad people, the Bible reveals that God is really concerned about repentant and unrepentant people. And that difference is huge!

PERSONAL CONFLICT

Author Ken Sande writes and speaks on the issue of conflict resolution. There is no situation where detecting sin is more difficult than in the midst of a conflict. Whenever you are engaged in a conflict, there is a strong inclination to judge other people's motives and actions and to excuse your own. In every conflict, there inevitably are behaviors from all parties that have contributed to the situation. Owning up to your part, no matter how small, has a way of opening the door for resolution and peace. Jesus said, "Blessed are the peacemakers." It is a sad commentary that Christians are quite often no better at resolving conflict than non-Christians. Christians should constantly be working toward repentance and peace. But too often, Christians refuse to give an inch in the midst of a conflict.

Owning up to our sin is incredibly challenging. We are constantly trying to twist our words, to apologize without really apologizing. We use phrases that start with "if," "but," or "maybe" to put conditions on our apologies. We like to leave escape clauses, possible ways out, room for a retraction or condition. It's very hard to apologize in concrete terms that leave no room for excuse or retraction.

Here's a good thought to consider—the sin I should be most upset about is my own!

IDOLATRY

At the end of the day, all sin is rooted in idolatry. The Bible makes it clear that the human heart is an idol-making factory. When we want something, it tends to take over our passions and our minds. We are quickly and easily driven by the desire to get what we want instead of seeking first the kingdom of God. That's why Jesus said to seek first the kingdom of God and that all other things would be added to us as well. What Jesus was saying is, "If your heart is in the wrong place, if your motives are incorrect, everything falls apart." It's not a sin to enjoy the blessings of God's creation, rather it's a sin to worship them and place them before God. It may sound like a subtle distinction, but it is a central theme of the Bible: pursue God first, and life works. Pursue things before God and life falls apart. The prophet Jonah said, *"Those who cling to worthless idols forfeit the grace that could be theirs."* *(Jonah 2:8)* When the good things of God's creation are turned into idols, they can destroy us. The good things of God, enjoyed in fellowship with God, are a deep blessing.

LEGALISM VS. LAWLESSNESS

Unrepentant sin typically takes root through one of two distortions of God's Word: legalism or lawlessness. Legalism is using God's law to justify yourself based on good works. Lawlessness is ignoring God's law and justifying yourself based on your motives and intentions. At face value, both distortions sound biblical. Legalism sounds good because the Bible talks about following God's laws. Lawlessness sounds good because the Bible talks about grace and mercy. The problem with each one is that they embrace one truth and neglect the other contrasting truth. Christian living is the challenge of keeping both of these in balance based on God's Word.

Here's the way it works. Plug in a life issue, any blessing in life, and you can ruin it by being legalistic or lawless. Take entertainment: television, movies, and music. A legalistic person starts to make extra rules beyond God's Word and imposes those rules on other people as a means to judge others and justify self. For example, a Christian cannot watch an R-rated movie. That might be a good guideline to consider, but it is not a moral law of God. Be careful not to get legalistic about it! But don't become lawless either. R-rated movies often contain immoral and ungodly content. To excuse it and act like it doesn't matter is a problem. To condone sexual immorality, violence, and cruelty is not good or pleasing to God. At the very least, immoral content must be viewed through a biblical lens. Sin and evil are a part of life. Movies that bring out challenging social issues are important. Christians can view morally-controversial material and join in the cultural debates about right and wrong. If all Christians withdraw from culture, they are removed from the debate. A good rule of thumb concerning any kind of media is to ask yourself, "Will this particular movie, song, etc. lead me into sin, or not, regardless of the rating?"

Living in a sinful world as a Christian requires godly discernment, what the Bible calls wisdom. Knowledge is useful, but without godly wisdom, it can lead to trouble. Godly wisdom gives us insight into what is good and what is evil—and gives us God's counsel about how to deal with sinful situations in God-pleasing ways.

CONFESSION – FORGIVENESS

For Christians, repentance and forgiveness become a way of life. Discerning our heart's intentions and detecting good and evil become a life skill given by God through the Holy Spirit. Christianity is black and white in many regards. God's moral Law, his Ten Commandments, are very clear—there are moral absolutes, right and wrong. But life also calls for discernment, how to apply those moral truths in difficult situations. Christian living is the art of applying God's moral law to your daily life. It's also learning how to apply God's grace in Christian life.

Forgiveness is the only real answer for sin. Sin can't be ignored. When we try to ignore sin and just move on, resentment, unforgiveness, animosity, lawlessness, legalism, and other sinful attitudes build up and the heart begins to harden. In the short term, ignoring sin may seem easier. But in the end, it is very destructive to relationships with God and with your neighbors. The art of confessing and forgiving is a tough one to learn. It can only be done by the power of the Holy Spirit, the Counselor! Only when we have experienced the unconditional grace of Jesus can we even begin to find the power to give that grace to others. In spite of the craziness of sinful mankind, God's resolve to love and forgive is unshakable.

PERSONAL REFLECTION

1. Read over the following Bible passages several times. Reflect on the words and consider what God is saying to you through them. In the space below, write down a few notes about your thoughts.

> "Blessed is he whose transgressions are forgiven, whose sins are covered. Blessed is the man whose sin the Lord does not count against him and in whose spirit is no deceit. When I kept silent, my bones wasted away through my groaning all day long. For day and night Your hand was heavy upon me; my strength was sapped as in the heat of summer. Then I acknowledged my sin to You and did not cover up my iniquity. I said, 'I will confess my transgressions to the Lord'—and You forgave the guilt of my sin." (Psalm 32:1-5)

"Have mercy on me, O God, according to Your unfailing love; according to Your great compassion blot out my transgressions. Wash away all my iniquity and cleanse me from my sin. For I know my transgressions, and my sin is always before me. Against You, You only, have I sinned and done what is evil in Your sight, so that You are proved right when You speak and justified when You judge. Surely I was sinful at birth, sinful from the time my mother conceived me. Surely You desire truth in the inner parts; You teach me wisdom in the inmost place . . . The sacrifices of God are a broken spirit; a broken and contrite heart, O God, you will not despise." (Psalm 51:1-6, 17)

"When the people heard this (the gospel), they were cut to the heart and said to Peter and the other apostles, "Brothers, what should we do?" Peter replied, "Repent and be baptized, every one of you, in the name of Jesus Christ for the forgiveness of your sins. And you will receive the gift of the Holy Spirit. The promise is for you and your children and for all who are far off—for all whom the Lord our God will call." (Acts 2:37-39)

2. Give some thought to conflicts you have with people in your life: a grudge, an unresolved conflict, or an ongoing broken relationship. Give serious thought to things you have done to contribute to the problem. How can you be more honest about owning up to your part, breaking down some of the walls, and bringing forgiveness and healing? Do you tend to struggle more with being legalistic—or lawless (immoral)? Think of issues that are the hardest for you—what can you do to apply God's wisdom?

3. Pray for God to give you his Holy Spirit of wisdom and revelation so that you might know him better.

CHAPTER 9

THE SIXTH CORE TEACHING
GETTING TO KNOW JESUS THROUGH THE LORD'S SUPPER

Intimate Communion with God

WHEN IT COMES TO MARRIAGE, there are two important aspects to making it work. The first, and most important is loving commitment and faithfulness to each other. The second is knowing and practicing healthy relational behaviors. Needless to say, without the first one, the second one really doesn't matter. The word intimacy means closeness. It is a risky thing to get close to another person. Physically it is risky to be close to another person, because they could harm you. The farther away you are, the safer you are. The same is true emotionally. If you open your heart and draw close to a person emotionally, you run the risk of that person leaving you or turning against you and hurting you deeply.

When you draw close to a person emotionally, you begin to share your fears, your weaknesses, your past hurts and pains. You open up about your insecurities and sensitivities. Once those are exposed, they are easily attacked. If someone with intimate knowledge of you turns against you, they can tell everyone your deepest secrets. That's risky! In spite of the risks that come with relationships, most people take the risk. That's probably because people are created with a deep need to love and be loved.

Of course, the greatest risk takes place when two people get married. God's plan for marriage was discussed in Chapter 2—a lifelong commitment to one person; a level of intimacy in heart, mind, and body that is reserved for only one person. That's why God's bare minimum law for male/female relationships commands us to not commit adultery. Adultery is the deepest relational wound a person can inflict on another person. It is total betrayal. God knows very clearly the risk involved in adultery and the pain it causes. And so he says very simply, and very plainly, "Don't commit adultery!"

One of my favorite Bible passages is one I mentioned earlier in the book: "Above all else, guard your heart, for it is the wellspring of life." (Proverbs 4:23) The heart is guarded when it is surrounded by unconditional, faithful, committed love. When that situation is in place, a relationship blossoms and grows and is richly blessed. Friends who are faithful, committed, and loving are incredibly powerful. And so is a marriage based on the same things!

I believe that's why God uses the analogy of the relationship of a bride and groom to compare with his relationship with his people, the Church. The ultimate place for a person's heart to be guarded is in a relationship with God through Jesus. God's love is completely faithful, unconditional, and totally committed to our well-being.

THE SACRAMENT OF THE LORD'S SUPPER

The Lord's Supper is the second sacrament, the second sacred act in which God connects his grace and forgiveness to a physical element. In the bread and wine of Holy Communion, God the Son is physically present and imparts the forgiveness of sins. There are two aspects of taking the Lord's Supper. The first and most important is the spiritual blessing that comes through the meal. The second is the practical side of communion: what it is and what God says about how it is to be administered in the Church.

PARTICIPATION IN A MEAL

The Lord's Supper finds its origins in a meal. When Jesus first gave his disciples the Lord's Supper, they were participating in an annual festival meal called the Passover dinner. In the Old Testament book of Exodus, God freed the people of Israel from slavery in Egypt by sending the ten plagues. The tenth and final plague was called the Passover. Each Israelite family was instructed to sacrifice a lamb. The blood of the lamb was spread over their doorpost to spare them from the angel of death, who would see the blood of the lamb and pass over the home, sparing them of God's judgment. Then each family was to prepare a special meal with the meat of the lamb and other specific items. Each food in the meal was a reminder of their enslavement in Egypt, and of God's work of delivering them. The Passover meal became a very holy meal for the people of Israel.

Jesus and his disciples were eating the Passover meal on the night that he was betrayed, arrested, and sentenced to die. Jesus told his disciples he was giving them a new meal for a new covenant. Jesus was the perfect Lamb of God who came into the world to shed his blood to atone for the sins of all mankind, and free us from our enslavement to sin. In this new meal, the bread is the body of Jesus and the wine is the blood of Jesus.

Eating a meal together with other people has more significance than just eating food to nourish your body. Eating a meal together is fellowship. We eat meals with people with whom we have a relationship. Inviting someone into your home to share a meal is a sign of friendship, of peace, and of fellowship. In the Lord's Supper, God gives us the very intimate setting of sharing a meal with Jesus. It is a sign of fellowship, of relationship, of friendship, and of peace with God. It is a meal rooted in God's work of salvation. It gives forgiveness of our sins and connects us to Jesus! Just as people don't make or accept dinner invitations without some thought, so this special meal asks us to consider what all is happening in this invitation from Jesus.

THREE DIFFERENT VIEWS OF THE LORD'S SUPPER

In the Christian Church, there are basically three different views of the Lord's Supper. The Catholic Church believes that the bread and wine of communion turn into (transubstantiation) the body and blood of Jesus. When you eat and drink, you are receiving two things—the actual body and blood of Jesus. The Catholic Church practices "closed communion"— in other words, only Catholics in good standing with the church are supposed to take communion in a Catholic Church. Likewise, Catholics are not supposed to take communion at non-Catholic churches.

The second view is held by most Reformed, Protestant, and Evangelical churches—it is the symbolic view of the Lord's Supper. Their teaching holds that the Lord's Supper is only symbolic. God is present in a spiritual way, like he is present in all places (known as his omnipresence). These churches believe there are two things present at the Lord's Supper—bread and wine. People who hold this position tend to emphasize the words of Jesus, "Do this in remembrance of Me." Most of these churches practice open communion—anyone is welcome. Since it is only a symbol, it isn't practiced as often. Some churches are careful and ask that only people who are baptized Christians participate.

The third view is held by the Lutheran Church and is called "real presence." This teaching asserts that Jesus is physically present in, with, and under the bread and wine. It is a mystery that defies human logic. People who hold to this teaching tend to emphasize the words of Jesus, "This is My body . . . This is My blood." The theme of God's physical presence is woven into several stories of the Bible. In the Old Testament, God dwelt physically over the tabernacle (a tent used for worship) in the form of a cloud. God inhabited the cloud. His physical presence was very real and very different than his spiritual presence everywhere. When a person eats the bread and wine of communion, mysteriously connected to the body and blood, Jesus is literally absorbed into your flesh. That may come across as rather strong, earthy language. But Jesus said these words, *"I tell you the truth, unless you eat the flesh of the Son of Man and drink his blood, you have no life in you."* *(John 6:53)* Pretty strong words! But they emphasize a critical spiritual truth: apart from being one with Jesus Christ, there is no life.

In Genesis 2:24, God said that a husband and wife would be united and become one flesh. That same verse is quoted later in the Bible by St. Paul: *"For this reason a man will leave his father and mother and be united to his wife, and the two will become one flesh.' This is a profound mystery—but I am talking about Christ and the Church." (Ephesians 5:31-32)* Clearly, the Apostle Paul is pointing out the intimate connection that exists between Jesus and his people. Nowhere is that close connection more intimately experienced than in the Lord's Supper.

PRECAUTIONS – GUIDELINES

When it comes to relationships, God set up boundaries for sexual relationships—the boundaries of marriage. Like a dam that holds back water and channels it to harness its power and energy, so marriage becomes a boundary that channels sexuality to be all God intended it to be. When experienced with only one person in a lifetime commitment of faithfulness, it can bring all the joy God intended. But when those cautions and guidelines are ignored, sex can become an extremely harmful thing.

Likewise with the Lord's Supper, God's Word provides some words of caution when it comes to communing with him! Read these words from St. Paul, *"Is not the cup of thanksgiving for which we give thanks a participation in the blood of Christ? And is not the bread that we break a participation in the body of Christ?" (I Corinthians 10:16)*

Just as there are moral and social norms surrounding the process of getting married, so there are some practices employed in communing in the

Church. Here are some guidelines used by congregations:

1. Are you a baptized believer and follower of Jesus?

2. Do you believe in the physical presence of the body and blood of Jesus in the Lord's Supper, in, with, and under the bread and wine?

3. Do you fear God's holiness and are you sincerely repentant of your sins? And do you trust only in Jesus Christ for the forgiveness of your sins?

4. Do you intend to turn from your sin and lead a life pleasing to God?

5. Do you believe the Bible is the inspired Word of God and submit your life to the authority of it?

6. Do you agree with the doctrinal confession of this congregation and its denomination? (The LCMS)

PHYSICAL AND SPIRITUAL REALITY

Jesus gives the Lord's Supper to be a rich spiritual blessing to his people. He knows that physical ceremonies and celebrations have a way of making invisible spiritual realities more tangible. He knows that participating in the sacraments provides a deep and meaningful assurance that your sins are forgiven, that you are a child of God, that your salvation is complete.

Married couples regularly and genuinely communicate their love for each other. It is important! We need daily assurance and affirmation. All human beings struggle with the uncertainties and anxieties of being in a relationship. Assurances are needed on a regular basis. That's what Jesus has given in his Supper—a participation in the redeeming work of Jesus.

What a gift God has given in the Lord's Supper, a meal of fellowship with Jesus and other Christians, assuring us that our sins are forgiven and that Jesus is with us!

FINAL THOUGHTS

"Now the Bereans were of more noble character than the Thessalonians, for they received the message with great eagerness and examined the Scriptures every day to see if what Paul said was true." (Acts 17:11)

In the New Testament, the Apostle Paul was called by Jesus to travel throughout the Roman Empire and to share the message of the gospel with the Gentiles. When he got to a city named Berea, he found a group of people who were eager to learn about God and took the task of finding the truth very seriously. That's a smart way to go about seeking God's truth: listen to good teaching, and then go study the Bible to make sure it all adds up. In other words, don't take it for granted; own it for yourself.

At the heart of this book is the desire to help people know Jesus. Like being introduced to a person you don't know, an introduction is only the beginning of a relationship. Maybe you have known Jesus as your Savior and Lord for a long time, and this book was just a good reminder of who Jesus is. Maybe you've practiced religion, but never really grasped what the gospel is all about. Or maybe the gospel is completely new to you. No matter where you are in your relationship with Jesus, it is my prayer that this book leads you to dig into another book— the Bible. Like the Bereans, the best thing to do is to open the Bible and see for yourself.

I will leave you with two final thoughts, both from God's Word. I hope you will meditate on them, and that through them, God's voice will speak clearly to you of his great desire for you to know him better. May the Good News of Jesus take you from knowing about Jesus to knowing Jesus personally—to a deep and genuine relationship with Jesus Christ.

Jesus prayed, *"Now this is eternal life: that they may know You, the only true God, and Jesus Christ whom You have sent." (John 17:3)*

"I keep asking that the God of our Lord Jesus Christ . . . May give you the spirit of wisdom and revelation so that you may know him better." (Ephesians 1:17)

PERSONAL REFLECTION

1. Read over the following Bible passages several times. Reflect on the words and consider what God is saying to you through them. In the space below, write down a few notes about your thoughts.

"While they were eating, Jesus took bread, gave thanks and broke it, and gave it to his disciples, saying, 'Take and eat; this is My body.' Then he took the cup, gave thanks and offered it to them, saying, 'Drink from it, all of you. This is My blood of the covenant, which is poured out for many for the forgiveness of sins.'" (Matthew 26:26-28)

"Wives, submit to your husbands as to the Lord. For the husband is the head of the wife as Christ is the head of the church, his body, of which he is the Savior. Husbands, love your wives, just as Christ loved the church and gave himself up for her to make her holy. In this same way, husbands ought to love their wives as their own bodies." (Ephesians 5:22, 25-26, 28)

2. Consider the closest relationships you have in life—your spouse, children, family, relatives, and good friends. What situations give you anxiety and cause you to do things that are harmful to the people you love? What are some ways you blame others instead of accepting responsibility for your own actions? What are some ways you could put aside your own needs in order to serve and love others unconditionally, which may break down some walls of hostility?

3. The next time you are taking communion in church, meditate on God's unconditional love for you, and pray for the Holy Spirit to help you love others unconditionally

Getting to Know Jesus

SMALL GROUP BIBLE STUDY
AND DISCUSSION GUIDE

SMALL GROUP BIBLE STUDY AND DISCUSSION GUIDE

THIS SMALL GROUP BIBLE STUDY and discussion guide is designed to be used by a group of 4-10 people who want to further discuss the concepts in this book and dig deeper into God's Word.

Note: The use of a study Bible will help you with questions you have about the Bible passages.

INTRODUCTION
Getting Started

1. Think of a person or even multiple people you know on a sincere, deep, and maybe even on an intense level. What were the main factors that allowed your relationship to deepen and become more meaningful?

2. Jesus says in Matthew chapter 6, "Where your treasure is, there your heart will be also." In what ways do you find Jesus' words in Matthew to be true in your own life? How would you describe your current level of contentment with what you treasure and where you are investing your life?

3. What is the difference between "knowing about Jesus" and "knowing Jesus." How can recognizing this difference shed new light on someone's understanding of Christianity? How can it help guide you in the process of growing in a deeper relationship with Jesus Christ?

4. What is your first impression of seeing the Six Core Teachings of the Bible as a way to know Jesus better?

Digging Deeper

Read Luke 7:36-50

1. What is the point of the story Jesus tells to the Pharisee?

2. Describe the difference between the Pharisee's relationship with Jesus and the woman's relationship with Jesus.

3. Why did the woman love Jesus more than the Pharisee?

4. What is this story teaching us about Jesus? What is it teaching us about sin and forgiveness?

Read Psalm 139

This Psalm helps us see that God already knows everything there is to know about us.

1. How does it make you feel that God knows you this well? Why?

2. What does this Psalm reveal to you about God – who he is, what he is like?

Read Colossians 1:15-20

This passage asserts that Jesus is the center of all creation.

1. In your own words, what is this passage saying about Jesus?

2. Which verse is the most helpful to you, why?

Connecting the Dots

1. Share the best thing you learned about Jesus in the introduction.

2. Describe your life journey especially in light of your faith and relationship with Jesus. Think of times you have been close to him, far from him, struggling with faith, strong in faith. Who has helped you in your walk of faith? What events in your life have been major influences on who you are and what you believe?

3. Where are you right now on your spiritual journey of faith?

4. Intimacy is one of the most special gifts God gives to us – physically, emotionally, and spiritually. With intimacy comes understanding and closeness within a relationship. In what ways do you find this to be true in your life?

5. We experience intimacy, depth, communication, identity, vulnerability, and commitment in relationships with others. In what ways can you experience these same gifts in relationship with Jesus?

CHAPTER 1

THE BIG PICTURE
An Explanation of the Gospel – The Six Core Teachings of the Bible

GETTING STARTED

1. Look at the list on page 21 about the differences between man-made religion and what God has revealed to us in the gospel. Are there any on the list that you have misunderstood? Explain.

2. Which of the six core teachings is the most interesting to you? Why?

3. If you died today, do you think you would go to heaven? Why or why not?

4. Try to summarize the message of the gospel in your own words in a sentence or two.

DIGGING DEEPER

Read Romans 3:20-28 and Ephesians 2:1-10

1. What is your first reaction to the message of these passages? What strikes you the most?

2. What do you think is the main point of these passages?

3. What do these verses have to say about doing good works to earn God's favor or to earn a place in heaven?

4. Is anyone good enough to earn a place in heaven? Explain.

5. What does the Bible say opens heaven to a sinner?

Read Luke 15:11-32

1. Describe the heart of the younger son based on his words and actions.

2. What is your reaction to how the father welcomes home the younger son? How does it make you feel?

3. Are you more like the younger son or the older son? Why?

4. What does this story reveal to you about the heart of God?

Read Luke 5:27-32

1. Why are the Pharisees frustrated by Jesus? What does this story reveal about the hearts and attitudes of the Pharisees?

2. What do you think Jesus is teaching in verses 31-32?

CONNECTING THE DOTS

1.   Share the best thing you learned about Jesus in chapter one.

2.   Do you find commitment to be something scary or remarkably refreshing and fulfilling? Explain. Jesus says in Matthew chapter 28, "And surely I will be with you to the end of the age." Reflect on the endless commitment of love from Jesus and rest in his unconditional faithfulness.

3.   What is your reaction to the idea of getting to know Jesus as the focus of being a Christian? What insights does that idea give you into being a Christian?

4.   What questions do you have at this point in your study? What is confusing to you?

CHAPTER 2

THE FIRST CORE TEACHING
GETTING TO KNOW JESUS THROUGH THE TEN COMMANDMENTS
God's Values – Ten Truths that Give and Govern Life

GETTING STARTED

1. Name a close friend and list some of the values that you share. How do those shared values strengthen your friendship?

2. In your life, do you feel the Ten Commandments are a burden and added weight on your shoulders, or do you feel they are a help to you? Why?

3. Are you generally a rule follower or a rule breaker? Explain. How much do you struggle with authority? Why or why not?

4. Which commandment in this chapter was the most interesting to you? Why? What does it reveal to you about God's heart? Why?

DIGGING DEEPER:

Read Psalm 19:7-14

The word "law" can also be interpreted as teachings/truths.

1. What does this passage tell us about God's truths? Which description is the most interesting or insightful for you? Why?

2. What do verses 12-13 tell us about the challenge of sinning against God's law?

Read Matthew 5:17-48

1. Jesus demands that we follow both the spirit of the law and the letter of the law. In other words, our actions and our intentions matter. What is your reaction to these words of Jesus?

2. What is your reaction to the level of obedience Jesus demands?

3. Verses 43-48 talk about loving your enemy as one of the distinguishing marks of the Christian faith. What is so radical about this principle? How is loving your enemy a reflection of what God has done for you?

Read Psalm 51 and Psalm 32

1. What do these passages tell you about the depth of our sinfulness and our need for God's mercy?

2. What verses capture your attention the most? Why?

CONNECT THE DOTS:

1. After reading this chapter, has your view on The Ten Commandments changed? Explain.

2. It is often easier to apply God's law to other people than it is to ourselves. How do these commandments help you look at your own heart? How do they help you love Jesus more?

3. "The worst sinner I know is me." What is your reaction to this quote? How does it affect your ability to treat others with grace?

4. The Bible shares three uses for God's perfect law: *As a* **curb** *(our conscience/natural instinct that tells us we are doing wrong; a way of correcting our way of life), a* **mirror** *(to help us realize our sinfulness and God's holiness), and a* **guide** *(being shown the best way to live for God)*. Have you encountered any of these uses of the law in your life? Explain. How have they helped you in your daily life?

5. Between gossip, slander, and hindering the truth, words have the ability to cause so much damage. At the same time, words also have the ability to lift up, encourage, and affirm others in what they do and who they are. Why is it so tempting to fall into the sin of talking negatively about others? Why is it so difficult to speak highly of others and see them as our Savior Jesus does? How can we stop ourselves from speaking negatively and begin to speak more highly of others and truly *"love your neighbor as yourself"*?

6. Sexuality and physical contact is one of the most extremely powerful human behaviors. It has the power to be beautiful and have meaning if used according to God's design, but it also has the power to tear relationships apart. In your life, how have you seen this at work?

7. What is the best thing you learned about Jesus in this chapter?

CHAPTER 3

THE SECOND CORE TEACHING
GETTING TO KNOW JESUS THROUGH THE APOSTLES' CREED – GOD'S IDENTITY

Part I – God the Father – Yahweh, Your Creator

GETTING STARTED

1. A gift can be anything from a toy to a relationship. Gifts come in all shapes, sizes, and prices – sometimes they are even priceless. What is the best gift you have ever received? What made this gift so special?

2. What are a few things in your life for which you are most grateful? Why?

3. In general, are you more content with your life, or are you frustrated and unsatisfied? Why?

4. How do you feel about seeing everything you have as a gift from God?

DIGGING DEEPER

Read Genesis 1:1-5, 2:1-3 and John 1:1-5, 14

The book of Genesis explains the genesis, or beginning, of all things. Everything that exists has its beginning in Genesis – except God, of course.

1. How did God create things?

2. What is John saying about Jesus in John 1?

3. What connections do you see between these two passages?

Read Luke 11:1-13

1. What is the main point of verses 9-13? What does this tell you about God the Father?

2. What do you think is the connection between Jesus teaching us how to talk to God and God's desire to bless us?

Read Psalm 19:1-6

1. What do you think is the main point of this passage?

2. What is the connection between God and his creation?

CONNECTING THE DOTS:

1. How does giving and receiving gifts allow us to understand God's heart?

2. *"He richly and daily provides me with all that I need to support this body and life."* What does it mean to put your trust and hope in God the Father to provide for you daily?

3. What was the best thing you learned about God in this chapter?

4. Share a few of your favorite places in creation. What do they reveal to you about God?

5. How do you feel about God relating to you like a father?

CHAPTER 4

THE SECOND CORE TEACHING
GETTING TO KNOW JESUS THROUGH THE APOSTLES' CREED – GOD'S IDENTITY

Part II – God the Son – Jesus Your Savior

GETTING STARTED

1. Do you like your name? Why or why not? What does your first and last name mean? Why did your parents choose your particular name?

2. Share a couple of people you think have a good name and reputation. Why do feel that way about them?

3. Can you think of a time when your reputation was damaged? Was it by your actions or by someone else's? Why is it so frustrating and painful to have your reputation damaged?

DIGGING DEEPER:

Read John 14:1-6 and Acts 4:12

1. The Bible reveals that faith in Jesus Christ as God's only Son as our Savior from sin is the only way to get to heaven. What do you think about that truth? Why do you think this message is offensive to many people?

2. It has been said that there are only two religions (or categories of religions):

    -   Christianity, which teaches that people are saved by God's grace because of the death and resurrection of Jesus which atones for our sin; and

    -   All other religions, which teach that people are saved by doing good works that earn them favor in God's eyes.

    -   Why is grace such a difficult concept for humans to accept? Why do we prefer our own good works over God's free grace?

Read Matthew 28:16-20

1. What do you think Jesus teaches in the words of verse 18?

2. In verse 19, why do you think Jesus clearly tells us the name of God?

Read I John 4:1-6

1. What criteria can we use to discern if a spirit is from the one true God?

2. This passage suggests that there is a true God and other false gods. Why do you think humanity invents or believes false messages about God?

3. Why do you think the message of the gospel of Jesus is hard for the world to believe?

CONNECTING THE DOTS

1. What have you learned in this chapter about sin and our need for a Savior from sin?

2. Jesus asked Peter, "Who do you think I am?" Ask yourself, "Who do I think Jesus is?"

3. Put into your own words why the death and resurrection of Jesus is so important.

4. What is the best thing you learned in this chapter about Jesus?

CHAPTER 5

THE SECOND CORE TEACHING
GETTING TO KNOW JESUS THROUGH THE APOSTLES' CREED – GOD'S IDENTITY

Part III - The Holy Spirit - Your Counselor and Comforter

GETTING STARTED

1. Share a time when a counselor or a good friend helped you see something about yourself that you didn't realize.

2. Why is getting feedback and input about ourselves so important? Why is it often difficult?

3. Why do you think we often need other people to help comfort us in difficult times?

DIGGING DEEPER

Read John 14:15-31 and John 16:5-16

In these passages, Jesus is telling his disciples that very soon his time on earth will be done. He explains that he will send the Holy Spirit to work in and through God's people.

1. In verse 26 – what does Jesus say is one work of the Holy Spirit? Why is this point so important?

2. Look on page 79 for Luther's explanation to the third part of the Apostles' Creed. What does this mean? After looking at the list of things the Holy Spirit does, how does that information help bring you peace? (John 14:27)

3. A counselor rarely has black and white answers to fix your problems. Instead, he or she asks questions, offers insights, and helps guide your thinking. How does that better help you understand the work of the Holy Spirit?

Read Acts 2:1-13, 14-36, 37-41 (the account of a day called Pentecost)

1. Look at 2:1-13. Why do you think the Holy Spirit comes in the form of a flame of fire? What do the two have in common? What does this imagery teach us about the Holy Spirit?

2. Read verses 14-36. Look closely at verses 22-24 and summarize in your own words what Peter is saying. Why is this so important?

3. Read verses 37-41. What do you think the phrase "cut to the heart" means in verse 37? Why do you think this message cut them to the heart? Why would this message still cut people to the heart today?

Read Ezekiel 37:1-14

In the Hebrew language, breath, wind, and spirit, are all the same word. Notice all the times those three words are used in this passage.

1. Why do you think God had Ezekiel preach to the bones as a way to bring them back to life? What was God revealing through this vision? What can we learn from this?

2. Read Ephesians 2:1-6 and John 5:24. How are these passages connected to the story in Ezekiel 37? Why do you think the Bible uses "resurrection" language to talk about coming to faith in Jesus Christ as your Savior?

CONNECTING THE DOTS:

1. God hates sin and separation from his people. He desires to be in an intimate relationship with us, but our actions and what happens in our lives often causes separation between God and us. What seems to separate and create distance between you and God?

2. How can you look for the Holy Spirit to be your counselor and comforter in your daily life?

3. How does the Holy Spirit help you to know Jesus better through your daily life?

4. What is the best thing you learned about the Holy Spirit in this chapter? Why?

CHAPTER 6

THE THIRD CORE TEACHING
GETTING TO KNOW JESUS THROUGH THE LORD'S PRAYER

Communicating with God

GETTING STARTED:

1. What are the main ways you communicate with family, friends, colleagues?

2. What is your greatest pet peeve when it comes to communication?

3. What is something you do that impedes communication with others?

4. What makes a person an effective communicator?

DIGGING DEEPER:

Read Matthew 6:5-15

1. What is Jesus saying to us about prayer in verses 5-8?

2. Why do you think Jesus gives us a list of things to talk to him about?

3. Which one of the phrases in the Lord's petition is the most meaningful to you? Why?

Read Ephesians 1:15-18 and Ephesians 3:14-21

1. What do you think it means when Paul says "that they eyes of your heart may be enlightened"?

2. Why do you think Paul's prayer for the Ephesians is to "know Jesus better"?

3. List the things Paul prays for in the second passage. Which is the most meaningful to you? Why?

4. How can you use these prayers for yourself and the people you know and love?

Read Matthew 7:7-12

1. What insights do you gain from verses 7-8 into Jesus' thoughts on prayer?

2. What is Jesus saying to you in verses 9-11?

3. How do these verses help you think about your own prayer life?

CONNECTING THE DOTS:

1. Do you enjoy serious and personal conversations, or are they a struggle for you? Why?

2. Who is someone easy to talk to about serious, deep, and personal subjects? What qualities does that person have that makes it easy for you to talk about serious subjects?

3. How would you characterize your conversations with Jesus? Serious? Frequent? Deep and meaningful? Common and ordinary?

4.   What is your prayer life like? When do you pray? Where do you pray? What resources do you use to help you? How does reading the Bible help your prayer life?

5.   What was the best thing you learned about Jesus in this chapter?

CHAPTER 7

THE FOURTH CORE TEACHING
GETTING TO KNOW JESUS THROUGH BAPTISM

Being Identified with and Connected to God

GETTING STARTED:

1. Share some of the most important commitments you have in life.

2. Why is commitment so meaningful and so difficult at the same time?

3. What do you worry about in life? What do you fear? Why?

DIGGING DEEPER:

Read Matthew 3:13-17

1. Baptism was a common religious ritual. A ceremonial washing was a physical action that reminded people of their need to be spiritually cleansed and for their sins to be washed away. Why do you think this ceremony was helpful to people?

2. Why do you think Jesus was baptized?

3. What do you think Jesus meant when he said, "To fulfill all righteousness"?

Read Matthew 28:16-20

1. Verse 17 says some of the disciples doubted. What do you think they doubted? Why did they doubt?

2. Why do you think Jesus tells his disciples to make more disciples by baptizing and teaching?

3. Why is it important that Jesus specifically identifies how the disciples should be baptized (in the name of the Father, Son, and Holy Spirit)?

Read Romans 6:1-7

1. What do you think it means to be baptized into the death and the resurrection of Jesus?

2. What does it mean to be united with Jesus?

CONNECTING THE DOTS:

1. Why do you think Jesus chose applying water as the action that would miraculously and mysteriously connect us to himself?

2. Think of some common "physical markings" that people use to convey what is important to them. Why are these helpful?

3. Martin Luther said that every morning when you wash your face you should remember your baptism. How can remembering and celebrating your baptism be helpful in your life of faith?

4. What is the best thing you learned about Jesus in this chapter?

CHAPTER 8

THE FIFTH CORE TEACHING
GETTING TO KNOW JESUS THROUGH CONFESSION AND FORGIVENESS

Genuine Repentance, Amazing Grace

1. Sometimes it is hard to be honest about our sin and vulnerable enough to share the darkest parts of our lives. In what ways do you find it hard or easy to be open about your struggles?

2. When was a time in your life that you opened up about your struggle with sin? How did that feel?

3. Why is it so difficult and frightening to be honest about our sins and weaknesses?

DIGGING DEEPER:

Read Psalm 130

1. What does this passage say about our need for forgiveness?

Read I John 1:8-10

1. What does this passage say about denying the fact that we are sinners?

Read Psalm 51

1. What do you think the writer means in verse 5 that he was sinful at birth, sinful from the time his mother conceived him?

2. What do you think the writer means in verse 6?

3. What do you think the writer means in verse 17?

Read Psalm 19:12-13

1. Why do you think the writer is particularly concerned about hidden sin and willful sins?

2. When someone willfully and repeatedly sins against you, what does it do to your relationship? Why?

Read Luke 24:44-49 and 1 Corinthians 15:3-4

1. What is the main message Jesus tells the disciples to share?

2. It is often said that the forgiveness of sins through the death and resurrection of Jesus is the central truth of the Bible and the Christian faith. What do you think that means?

CONNECTING THE DOTS:

1. Why do you think all human beings have such a hard time owning up to their sins?

2. Why is grace and mercy so powerful, especially when it is undeserved?

3. Why is daily repentance so important in the life of a Christian? How do you practice daily repentance?

4. What is the best thing you learned about Jesus in this chapter?

CHAPTER 9

THE SIXTH CORE TEACHING
GETTING TO KNOW JESUS THROUGH THE LORD'S SUPPER

Intimate Communion with God

GETTING STARTED:

1. Why do you think some people are more comfortable than others with getting close to another person? Are you comfortable being close to other people? Why or why not?

2. Why do you think marriage can be the source of great joy, and also of great pain?

3. How close is your family? How open are you about your love and affection for each other?

DIGGING DEEPER

Read Ephesians 5:21-33

1. What does it mean for two people to submit to one another? Why is this such a powerful experience? What happens when a husband and wife don't submit to each other?

2. What do you think verses 31-32 mean?

3. Why is the phrase "one flesh" such a powerful image of intimacy?

4. Why do you think God uses marriage as a picture of the relationship he desires to have with you?

Read Matthew 26:26-29

1. Why do you think Jesus said, "This is my body... this is my blood"?

2. How does eating and drinking the body and blood of Jesus, in, with, and under the bread and wine, result in a "one flesh" union?

Read 1 Corinthians 11:17-34

1. Why do you think Paul is so concerned about people participating in the Lord's Supper without proper respect and reverence?

2. What do you think Paul means in verses 27-29?

3. What do these verses tell you about the practice of taking communion in church?

CONNECTING THE DOTS

1. Why do you think Jesus gave us a meal as one of the most sacred acts for Christians to do regularly?

2. Why is the real presence of Jesus in, with, and under the bread and wine such an important and powerful truth?

3. What do you do to prepare to take the Lord's Supper? What do you think about and pray about as you take the Lord's Supper?

4. What is the best thing you learned about Jesus in this chapter?

To order additional copies of *Getting to Know Jesus*, go to:

www.TenthPowerPublishing.com